Praise for
The Operation 36 Golf Program

"My son started this program at 7 years old and has progressed through the levels of the curriculum and on-course yardages over the last 10 years while making some life long friendships along the way. What I've observed is his love of playing the game of golf has increased every year he's been in the program. He is now to a point where he is motivated to come out to the course on a regular basis, has set his own goals to play in college, and is working hard to reach that. As a parent. I couldn't ask for more."

— **Jeff Howard - PARENT**

Simply the best, most complete coaching program out there and has made our facility better, along with my own coaching."

— **James Salt, PGA, Manchester, UK - GOLF COACH**

"Our family is so thankful for the Operation 36 program! With most sports for youth, the structure or curriculum is unclear (if it exists), but with Operation 36, you can see a clear path for being a life-long golfer. Most of all, this program has provided confidence to our son/or daughter, by setting and achieving goals. Not to mention, our family has a sport that we can all play together."

— **Justin Miller - PARENT**

"To say that Operation 36 has been life changing would be an understatement! It's given me a clear roadmap to becoming an extremely busy full-time instructor and now Director of Instruction. No doubt our golf club's overall health and engagement is largely due to our programming options with Operation 36."
— **Scott Erdmann, PGA, Oregon, USA - GOLF COACH**

"Operation 36 has provided me a community where I can decompress, meet new friends, and improve my game. It's not super competitive as I'm not trying to beat my friends. Rather, we are all working together to try to beat the course (shoot 36), which is a great way to build camaraderie. Getting me on the golf course and playing in the 9-hole events on a regular basis has been so helpful for me to take what I learn in class and apply that on the course. I am now confident enough in my game and understanding how to play that when someone asks me to play golf in a charity scramble or casual round. I'm 100% in!"
— **Mary Ellen Perry - LADIES ACADEMY**

"It just makes sense, have success from the closer yardages and as I improve with the help of my coach and encouragement of my classmates the game gets more challenging. Basically, I hold the keys to how hard I want to make this game. Why would I start any other way?"
— **Rodney Lewis - MENS ACADEMY**

"Operation 36 is just a way better structured program. The progression through the yardages and being play-based, everything is focused around playing golf."
— **William McGirt - PGA Tour Winner and Op36 PARENT**

"I absolutely love the program. It has been a huge success with my programs. What's the coolest part is it can be used for everyone. Our ladies group loves it."
— **Meredith Lobeck, LPGA/PGA, California, USA - GOLF COACH**

"Operation 36 has made a fantastic impact on Griffin Golf and our community. We have the privilege of teaching at 3 different facilities and share this program with all women and juniors! We enjoy creating golfers and getting everyone on the course shooting 36 or better for 9 holes. We have over 200 students in our community and the upgraded app has been fantastic getting the golfers engaged in the program! Operation 36 provides a road map for our students and keeps them working on their game all year long."
— **Sara Griffin, PGA, Washington, USA - GOLF COACH**

HOW TO CREATE A JUNIOR GOLFER

THE OPERATION 36® MODEL

The most effective road-map for beginner golfers
to have fun becoming a skilled golfer

RYAN DAILEY
& MATT REAGAN

Copyright © 2022 by Operation 36 Golf

All rights reserved. Including the right to reproduce this book or portions thereof in any form whatsoever. For information address Operation 36 Golf Publishing Department, PO Box 735, Buies Creek, NC 27506.

For information about special discounts for bulk purchases, please contact Operation 36 Golf at 919-746-7255 or support@op36golf.com.

Operation 36 Golf can bring Ryan and Matt to your live event. For more information or to book an event, contact Operation 36 Golf at 919-746-7255 or support@op36golf.com.

Book Illustrations and cover by Melissa Duffy
Book Design by AJ Reimann
Developmental editing by Amy Boehnert

First Printing: October 2022

How to Create a Junior Golfer
The Operation 36 Model: The most effective road-map for beginners to have fun becoming a skilled golfer.

ISBN: 9798403939614

Printed in the United States of America

www.operation36.golf

HOW TO CREATE A JUNIOR GOLFER

The Operation 36 Model: The most effective road-map for beginners to have fun becoming a skilled golfer

This book is dedicated to those who have never held a club before, and those who have the honor of guiding those who have never held a club before, into playing what we think is the greatest game in the world – the game of golf.

Contents

Foreword by William McGirt
Introduction

Chapter 1: Why Golf?
Chapter 2: If They Don't Play, They Won't Stay
Chapter 3: The Operation 36 Development Model
Chapter 4: Finding the Right Level of Challenge
Chapter 5: The Big Picture is Made of Small Steps
Chapter 6: The "Secret Sauce" to Keeping your Junior Motivated
Chapter 7: Why This System Works
Chapter 8: How to Properly Develop a Junior Athlete
Chapter 9: The Role of Parents
Chapter 10: Next Steps

Additional Resources for Parents
Appendix
Notes
About the Authors

FOREWORD
By William McGirt, PGA Tour Winner

I play golf for a living and have been since 2004. After a handful of years on the mini tours, I broke through in 2010 to earn my tour card at Q school for the 2011 season. I've been fortunate enough to play in all four majors, with my best finish being a tie for 10th at the 2016 PGA Championship and a tie for 22nd at the Masters in 2017. I have been ranked as high as No. 38 in the world and got my first PGA Tour win at the Memorial Tournament in Ohio in 2016. (Shedloski, 2016)

William and his family with Jack Nicklaus after winning the Memorial Tournament. Photo: Getty Images

As you can probably imagine, I have traveled a lot and seen a lot since turning professional in 2004. Before 2004, I was a collegiate golfer in South Carolina, and prior to that, a junior golfer in North Carolina. I have seen, learned about, and experienced most every golf program imaginable. I've been making mental notes along the way on what I would want a program to have when my kids were born and I wanted to get them into golf.

When it came time to put my kids in a golf program a few years ago, I knew that I wanted something that was centered around playing on the golf course. I had seen enough of the traditional programming over the years in my travels to know I wanted something different. I knew that keeping players away from the golf course and playing was not the recipe for long term success. Lining them up on the driving range to hit balls and playing games at the practice facility is great, but it's missing something, something very important – what I would say is the most important piece.

It's missing what got me hooked on the game: playing on the course on a regular basis. By playing on the course, I became curious as to what I needed to do to improve. That motivated me to practice more and play more, and when you do that, it's a recipe for success. And the more I was at the course, the more friends I made. It was a great environment for me to grow up in.

I was very fortunate that when it was time for my boy to get a taste of the game, our local golf pro, Kevin Britt in South Carolina was running Operation 36. I'd never heard of the program before, but after discussing it with him, I was all in. The progression of the yardages made sense to me and I was ecstatic that he was getting on the course right from the start of his journey. He was competing against himself and the course which I've always felt that competition at the right time and in the right way is the fuel that lights the fire for so many.

It was pretty simple. Start close to the hole, and the goal is to shoot 36 or better for nine holes and then back up when you reach that goal. The weekly coaching with Coach Kevin is centered around having fun, making friends, games in class and working through a fundamental curriculum that gives them the skills to have success when they play in the bi-weekly nine hole events to try to beat 36. When I'm on the road, I can log into the app and see what they are working on and their progress.

A quick story of our first few experiences that may help you. My son was in his second or third nine-hole event and needed to finish with a 4 and a 4 on the last two holes to beat 36. I was caddying for him, and he was at the age where he was just having fun on the course with some new friends. He lost concentration at the end of the round as kids his age do and he finished with a 5 and a 7. He added up the score at the end and was surprised that he had a chance to beat 36, as he shot 40. He looked at his scorecard with Coach Kevin and figured out that he just needed to putt a little better.

As we left the scoring table, he said some words I'll remember for some time. "Daddy, I want to go to the putting green and practice my putting, I didn't putt very well today." I didn't say anything to him. I didn't drag him to the putting green. He was motivated to do it on his own based on the environment he was in. I happily jumped in the golf cart and drove to the putting green and watched while he practiced. The next time we went out, he putted much better and beat 36.

He was hooked. He learned a valuable lesson that he would have never learned if he was in a program where all he did was hit balls on the range or play games on the practice facility. He learned about work ethic and goals. He learned that if you want to get better at something you need a goal, and you need to work towards that goal. That goal for him was 36 and he worked on his skills to improve so he could achieve that goal. He also had the support of his coach, who also worked with him in class on his putting, as they both knew which area they needed to work on to have a direct impact on his next round.

Fast forward a few years and my son uses the lessons he learned back with Kevin on a daily basis in all areas of his life. Yes, he still loves golf and is progressing in his skills alongside his friends at the course. I'm certainly excited about that. In addition, he approaches his school work, baseball and other activities he does with an understanding that you need to work on your skills to improve them. I firmly believe that the foundation of that understanding came from his first experience with golf in the Operation 36 program.

As a parent, we are hoping our kids find an activity that they fall in love with and want to put in the work to improve. Many of us don't necessarily care what activity it is, we just want them to be passionate about something other than their devices. My wife and I are no different. If they choose golf, great. If they choose a musical instrument, coding, baseball or another sport, that is fine too. We just want them to be passionate about something.

It is our duty and responsibility as parents to put them in environments that give them the best chance to develop this passion. I firmly believe that the Operation 36 program is the best environment for someone to fall in love with playing the game of golf and developing a passion for a lifetime. I hope you enjoy reading "How to Create a Golfer" and strongly consider finding a program in your area to enroll your child into and yourself if you are looking to learn the game as an Adult.

If they don't play, they won't stay.

William McGirt
PGA Tour Winner

Introduction

In the late fall of 2014, our golf coaching season had just come to an end. The thick, bright green Bermuda grass had turned brown and a cool breeze let us know that winter would soon be here. We picked up the final pieces of equipment from our last class, then collapsed in the chairs in the golf pro shop. We were physically exhausted from the previous season.

We had just finished our fourth full year of coaching golf programs, and by all measures, it had been a success. We had worked seven days a week for years to grow a golf program in one of the most remote areas of the country.

Our little town had barely enough people to surpass the 2,000 mark for the 2010 census – a small town by anyone's standards. Each year our golf academy had grown, and though we were tired, the momentum was gaining.

Or so we thought…

Despite putting every single penny and every ounce of energy we had into creating the very best Junior Golf Program we could deliver, something went wrong.

Just before Christmas, we received a call. To our disappointment, we learned that a Junior Golfer would not be returning in the new year. When you own a business and you are putting everything you have into it, the sting of rejection hurts!

But we would learn that we would not experience that sensation one time, but 40 times before our next season began! Yes, 40 families had made the decision not to return to our golf academy in the new year.

We had the kind of experience that you have likely read about, perhaps a "dark night of the soul," where you begin to question everything!

"Didn't the families love our golf coaching?"
"What went wrong?"
"Why didn't we see this coming?"
"Can the coaching business survive to provide for our families?"

As you can imagine, this was a painful experience. In addition to the barrage of rejection, concern for the financial viability of our program, we were baffled as to what was really going on.
Why were so many Juniors leaving golf?

We had done what we were trained to do as golf professionals and even added to it. We created amazing experiences and games to motivate our players on a daily basis. We used video game-like tools such as points, badges and leaderboards. We brought out large props, piñatas, footballs, soccer balls and colorful gym equipment. We were really good at motivating or engaging our players because of a short-term goal, task or reward in class. Later we learned this short-term focus is exactly why we had failed.

We were so focused on making sure each and every day was a Disney World-type experience that we lost focus on the long-term goal: helping our players fall in love with playing the game of golf. We completely missed the target of providing an environment for our players that intrinsically motivated them, where the activity of playing golf on the course is fun and exciting, regardless of the reward.

We had a choice to make over that winter.

We could have quit and decided that there was no way to make it work. Or we could lick our wounds and determine a better way to teach a beginner to play golf.

Fortunately for us, we had incredibly supportive families that wanted to see us succeed. They allowed us to give this another try, and possibly fail, while requiring even more of our time and financial resources.

Because we had that support from our spouses, we were able to move forward into the unknown. We set our temporary defeat aside, and determined to solve this one question– "What is the best way to introduce a beginner to golf so that they want to play throughout their lifetime?"

We knew that if we could answer this question, it would have far-reaching implications. If we could really find the best way to share golf with a beginner, we could begin to change the trajectory of the decades-old decline in golf participation.

We were just naive enough to believe that if we could solve this one problem, we might just change the course of history for golf.

Chapter 1: Why Golf?

As a parent, you have probably attended a number of sports events, practices and try outs for your child. If you take a closer look at many youth sports, you will likely notice one interesting fact.

For many youth activities, you will often find children waiting...

Waiting in line for their turn...
Waiting on the bench...
Waiting on the sidelines...

While you signed them up for sports so that they would be active, you notice that much of the practice is waiting.

If you have ever had your child sit on the bench for most of the game, you know that waiting can be painful. And you hope it's not a traumatic story that they will share on a therapist's couch one day!

This is one of the countless reasons that we see golf as the perfect sport for youth. Just consider the fact that everyone can participate in golf. No matter your size, shape, gender or physical ability–everyone with a set of clubs can play.

You will also see that there is no "sitting on the bench" or waiting for a long time to participate. Despite its reputation for being exclusive, it is truly the most inclusive sports available to kids.

Beyond youth sports, giving your child the gift of golf is a gift that could last a lifetime. While you won't see many 70 or 80 year olds on a basketball court or football field, you will most certainly find them on the golf course.

Not only that, it is a sport that gets your kids outdoors. Whether they are at a lesson, practicing at the range or playing on the course, golf gets your child off a screen and into nature.

Many golfers pick up social skills because they chat with their peers and coach throughout the lesson and on the course. They pick up etiquette and learn to communicate and work with adults.

Finally, having a grasp of golf can be useful later in life if they choose to enter the business world. Many business deals have been negotiated on the course, and it still remains the sport of business.

So with so many positives, why isn't golf the number one choice for youth across the country?

But Golf Does Have One (Big) Problem

What if we told you that the numbers are showing that over 98% of people who try golf will quit before they actually become a competent golfer who will play for life?

Sadly, it's true.

The National Golf Foundation reported that there were over 12 million new golfers introduced to the game from 2015 to 2020, yet our actual total golfer count has only risen by 200,000 in that same time frame. That's right – for every 100 people introduced to the sport, 1.6 of them actually became a golfer.

As you can clearly see in the numbers, the way that golf is traditionally taught is flawed. It is so flawed that if it isn't corrected, the sport is in danger of disappearing over the long term. (Matuszewski, 2022)

Without a plan to help the beginner, golf is a complex, intimidating, unclear game that leaves many feeling lost and frustrated.

> "For every 100 players introduced to the sport, 1.6 turn into a golfer."

At Operation 36, we use the term "black hole" as a metaphor to define this threshold that we need to get beginners through to become confident golfers who love the sport. This is the period of time after someone is interested in golf, but before they are confident enough to go out on their own and know how to improve.

From our perspective, this is somewhere around a 26 handicap, or someone who can break 50 for nine holes (100 for 18 holes) on a standard-length course. Why? Breaking 100 for 18 holes is a huge milestone for golfers. It gives them the confidence they can play with almost anyone at any course without embarrassing themselves.

So how do we get golfers through the 'black hole' phase? We do this by giving beginners and golf coaches a clear, motivating path from beginner to par golfer.

We do this by creating milestones for the beginner golfer to achieve that are exciting, and are matched to their skill level.

We do this by making their day-to-day actions motivating every step of the way. We do this by immersing our beginners in the best learning environment possible and building the best team around this player to help guide them.

The process of becoming a golfer should be fun and motivating. It truly does not have to be a frustrating experience!

This book is about giving everyone a better plan to get started on the right track. Every beginner deserves to enjoy their journey, improve, and play the sport for a lifetime.

Traditional Golf Programs Are Falling Short

The best way we can characterize traditional golf programs is like waking up one day and saying, "We are going to get in a car and travel from New York to Los Angeles without a map or using the GPS on our cell phone or car!"

Getting started on the trip could be exciting and you are full of energy. However, without the map or GPS, after a few miles, it begins to get a bit complex. You probably would start to feel lost and uncertain as soon as you leave your hometown.

There would certainly be some frustration and anxiety as you travel down the road. You may start to ask questions like, "Why are we heading west again?" or "What was the purpose of this?"

At some point you would probably forget why you started, thinking, "This was a bad idea!" and turn back.

If you actually persevere and make it to your destination, it is a guarantee that if you had a clear destination, a GPS to follow, and a map if you got stuck, you could have gotten there much sooner and had enjoyed the journey a lot more! The problem with traditional beginner golf programs is there is no long-term plan. There is no destination. There is no roadmap.

If you want to learn the sport, the common program is usually a drop-in, game-based camp or clinic, or private lessons that may introduce you to the sport and focus on short-term fun, but lack purpose and a plan to actually turn you into a skilled golfer.

If you go to 10 different golf professionals and ask, "How do you take a beginner and turn them into a skilled golfer?" you will get 10 different answers. In almost every other sport, there is a common, structured, motivating, and clear plan. Think Karate or Gymnastics to name just two.

Not in golf.

You wouldn't send your son or daughter to a school with no curriculum, grade levels, standards, or a graduation would you? Of course not. It wouldn't be effective at all.

Developmental Golf Programming is the Future

A developmental golf program, quite simply, has a complete plan to follow to take someone from a beginner to a skilled golfer. There is a clear starting point and a clear destination. Along that journey, there will be checkpoints and milestones to know we are on track. There will be education to guide you and a supporting team who are there to help if you get stuck along the way.

If done right, everyone on this journey understands the plan before you start the trip. We all know the actions we need to take to get there, no one ever feels lost, we can make our day to day actions motivating, and we can actually see ourselves progressing towards our destination.

If we get off track, we will have some principles to follow to keep us in control and help us get back on the right path. Even though we will have our good days and bad days, we persevere and it actually becomes a very enjoyable and memorable experience.

If you haven't guessed yet, Operation 36 is a developmental golf program. We are looking forward to sharing with you the components of the Operation 36 Model and what we have learned over the past 13 years working with juniors and adults to help turn them into skilled lifelong golfers.

This framework and these lessons have accumulated from the collaboration with thousands of golf professionals who are delivering the Operation 36 Program and using the model and technology to create skilled lifelong golfers on a daily basis.

You will learn all the pieces to the puzzle that are required to get better, to make the journey fun, and have a clear picture to know you are on the right track.

This book is your plan for your Junior. It will give you the mindset to know the core actions you are working on and the environment you are in will work so you never feel lost and you see small progress from day one of your golf journey.

It will also show you how to make golf improvement fun every step of the way. It is the foundation that a golf development journey is built on.

Becoming a Golfer: In their Own Words

Matt Reagan, PGA

I started golf late. When I was 16 years old, I was tired of participating in track and field as my third sport. Let's just say it wasn't that fun to be looking at the backs of others during the 100-yard dash.

My high school physical education teacher and golf coach Steve Thompson recommended that I try playing golf. Steve gave me a set of clubs and took me to the Pinnacle State Golf Club, our school's home course, for my first practice.

We were already in season and the team had a match that day. The plan was once the match went off, I would get some instruction from Steve to begin my golf journey.

When we arrived, we learned that only three players from my team were able to make the match. You need four to have an official match against another school.

Steve looked at me and said, "Well, Matt, the best way to learn is to play, so you are playing." So my first nine holes and formal golf experience came right then – playing a nine-hole high school golf match at the age of 16!

I will never forget how anxious, embarrassed, and frustrated the first hole made me. In front of about 20 people, I topped every golf shot and stayed in the trees on the left hand side of the hole the entire way to the green. Thank goodness I had a teammate, Marshall, with me who was experienced. He guided me and encouraged me.

I will never forget how happy I was when I got the ball on the first green. I walked over to the ball, and set down my entire bag right in the center of the green. The huge smile on my face met Marshall's, who came over slowly and said, "You can't put the bag on the green! Pick it up and set it in the rough."

It was like a final jab of embarrassment! I finished the hole, and although feeling mortified and overwhelmed, there was a sense of accomplishment. I actually finished my first golf hole!

Looking back now, that was quite an introduction to the game, and it was probably a blessing that it happened. As embarrassing as it was, playing the game first and going through that experience motivated me to want to improve and actually finish nine holes with a reasonable score.

Over the next three years, I continued to receive guidance from my golf coach, Steve Thompson. In the winter, he would let me come over and hit balls into a net he had set up in his basement. He gave me tons of golf books to read. We would videotape my swing with a VHS recorder and plug it into a tv to try to figure out what to work on next. I played nine holes almost every day during the golf season because that was free for me as a member of the school golf team.

By the time I graduated high school, I had the ability to shoot even par (36) for nine holes from the white tees at Pinnacle.

What I have learned is that getting into golf does not have to be as embarrassing as my first experience. There can be a plan or model for you to follow that actually works. There wasn't a plan for me or my coach to follow. There were so many days we felt completely lost and I really didn't believe that the work I was putting in was going to work to turn me into a skilled golfer.

Why did we write this book?

This book is your plan for your Junior. It will give you the mindset to know the core actions you are working on and the environment you are in will work so you never feel lost and you see small progress from day one of your golf journey.

It will also show you how to make golf improvement fun every step of the way. It is the foundation that a golf development journey is built on. On to Chapter 2…

Chapter 2: If They Don't Play, They Won't Stay

With our Junior Golf Program on the brink of failure, we decided that we had to get to the bottom of what was really going on. Why were some juniors staying, and loving the program, but so many more ready to leave the game?

When we compiled a list of all the golfers who were staying in our program, we realized that they all had one thing in common.

These juniors who stayed played on the course with family members and had signed our practice book that showcased that the junior practiced/played at the facility when we were not in session.

Could it be that simple?

The ones who were in love with the game, and interested in continuing in golf were the only ones who were actually playing on the course. We knew we had to find a way to get golfers on the course in the program.

But then it hit us like a brick wall ... it is just hard to get a beginner golfer on the course. No wonder we avoided it! There was no easy and clear way to integrate this into our program.

So for the next twelve months, we explored every way possible to figure out a motivating, timely, and clear way to get a beginner to play 9 holes on the course.

From using the forward tees, to playing scrambles. They all took too long to play 9 holes or would be a soul-crushing experience for a Junior and parent to play on the course.

This hard lesson and a year of trial and error is what ultimately led to us developing the Operation 36 Development Model. We were able to figure out how to help a beginner become comfortable playing 9 holes and getting connected to the "real game".

A mantra was born (thank you William McGirt): "If they don't play ... they won't stay"

As we learned early on, classes and games aren't enough to create a golfer. They are important and you should have fun and engaging classes, but they aren't enough. They will only keep a junior or adult engaged for the short-term, but at some point, they need to learn to play the actual game and have a plan to improve for the long-term.

Look at every other sport! When you are learning how to swim, you get in the pool. When you are learning to play baseball, you get on the field and play against other teams. But with golf, beginners are actively encouraged to NOT PLAY the actual game?!

We avoid it at all costs. Yet we complain when rounds are down and the facility is struggling? It is time we stop avoiding getting beginners on the course, and we start embracing it.

Playing Golf Backwards?

In order to teach golf in a way that would be motivating for the long run, we decided to start golfers close to the hole, rather than at the tee box.

We began teaching golf backwards?
Yes!

As simple as it sounds, starting 25 yards from the hole allows anyone, regardless of size, strength, talent or experience to have success on the course.

So we created a plan to teach Juniors to play golf starting just 25 yards from the hole. Once the player could shoot 36 or better while playing 9 holes from 25 yards, they would graduate to the next level, which is 50 yards from the hole. As the golfer improves, she graduates levels and moves closer and closer to the tee box.

We will dive into the specifics of this model in the following chapter, but this first step, albeit *backwards,* was the most monumental in discovering the right way to create a golfer.

So it's Just That Simple? Start Closer to the Hole?

Well, not exactly!

As we have learned since 2015 when we created the *model*, there is so much more involved in creating a golfer, but it is a solid place to start.

A *program* needs to be built with the most effective tools to support a player and coach through this journey. These tools must not only support the player and coach, they must help foster an environment at the course amongst all participants that you are working together for a common goal.

Once everyone is aware of the common goal, a very motivating and supportive environment emerges. A supportive, engaging environment is critical for the long-term success of any sport.

More than a Swing

Playing golf is more than just learning how to swing a club and hit a ball. Please take a moment and let that sink in.

Yes, playing golf is a lot more than just learning how to swing a club and hit a ball. When we first started out as coaches, we thought if we taught someone how to swing and hit a ball they would naturally move over to the course and start playing. *Sadly, as you have learned already, that did not work out for us.*

Falling in love with playing the game of golf!

Romance Stage 36 Precision Stage

Figure 1: We would argue that the most challenging stage to help a golfer is the initial introduction to the sport (Romance Stage). How do you put a player in an environment to help them to fall in love with playing the game of golf?

Guiding someone to be comfortable in playing the game of golf involves a player learning the rules, etiquette and strategy in addition to swinging and hitting a ball.

Rules refer to how the game is played. Golf etiquette refers to the unofficial rules and practices designed to make the game safe and enjoyable. Finally, golf strategy encompasses everything from what club to hit, how hard to hit it, where to place your ball on your first shot to give you the best chance on your second shot, and so on.

A golfer who only knew how to swing the club would be completely lost on the basics of where to stand when someone else is hitting, where to hit the ball when it is their turn, what to wear to the course, how to play a hole or how to schedule a tee time to play with friends.

At one point, our team here at Operation 36 Headquarters listed out all of the different items someone would need to be aware of when playing golf. We stopped once the list got over 60!

Twenty two of the items were things someone would need to know before they even arrived at the course. No wonder people get frustrated when they try to learn to play the game, we need to make this process easier.

To keep this simple and motivating, using the Operation 36 Development Model encompasses all of this and more. That is what we will be sharing with you in future chapters. If someone follows the Operation 36 program and plays regular nine-hole events, he or she will learn how to play the game within the first couple of times on the course.

Sure, the playing of the game and improving your skills will take some time. But the new golfer will soon see the bigger picture and understand that there is a path forward to becoming a skilled golfer.

Becoming a Golfer: In their Coaches Words

Heather Henry – Began Operation 36 at 7 Years Old

Coach: Luc McCaw, PGA – Essex Golf & Country Club, Windsor, Ontario, Canada

Heather Henry started her golf journey alongside her older sister, Meredith, with the encouragement of their grandfather. Heather began at age 7 and for her first couple of years in golf, she sporadically participated in traditional camps and clinics.

After a couple of years, although Heather had attended clinics and been at the golf course quite often, she had never actually played her own golf ball on the golf course. At this point, Heather was enjoying her time at the golf course, but was still very much a recreational junior just sampling the sport.

In 2017, at 9 years old, Heather joined Operation 36. Heather's first on-course Operation 36 experience was shooting a 53 in Level 1 – 25 yards. This on-course experience was a motivator, and just two weeks later, she shot a 35 on her second attempt to advance. Level 2 didn't come quite so easily – she made six attempts before breaking through in August of that same year. This is where Heather's Level 3 – 100 yards journey began. Heather made, in total, 23 attempts at Level 3 from August 2017 to August 2019.

In my experience at our academy, Level 3 is where a lot of our developing juniors often meet their challenge point, where the journey becomes more difficult, and this was definitely true for Heather. However, she embraced the challenge over those 23 attempts and knew that when she was struggling…she was learning. You could say she, 'struggled on purpose.'

Heather and her sister have made a network of friends at the golf course through the Operation 36 program. They can be found playing the golf course and practicing at the practice facility outside of our regularly scheduled programming.

Heather embraced all aspects of Operation 36 – she was motivated by the leveling up process (mastery of skill objectives), both encouraged and was encouraged by her Operation 36 peers, and loved the on-course journey. After two years and 23 attempts, Heather shot a 35 in Level 3 in August of 2019. The lessons learned in overcoming that challenge point were elemental to her continued growth and success.

There were undoubtedly tough or disappointing days along the way. Ultimately the delayed- gratification of overcoming the challenge had supercharged her appetite for the game of golf.

Operation 36 taught Heather that challenge and failure can be an asset when what you're trying to do is improve and learn. Heather's interest, passion and work ethic continues to grow as she has become a very avid and skilled junior golfer at our club and in our community.

She is now representing our club at events, playing regional junior golf tournaments, and will be playing for her high school golf team this season! She is always looking for the next challenge, an invaluable attribute in golf and in life.

Chapter 3: The Operation 36 Development Model

What we learned from our early failure is that if we want Juniors to stick with golf, they need to see the bigger picture. To be willing to practice over weeks, months and years, they have to understand where they are going and how it serves a larger goal.

In our early days, that meant that we were playing games with players at the practice facility, but preventing them from playing on the course. Now we understand that every beginner needs to be on the course to be able to see how each activity helps them improve.

Certainly, if someone is very young, this will not be the case. However, at some point, we think earlier than later, a player needs to know why they are learning what they are learning. It makes them curious and engages the brain to want to learn more.

The most effective learning environment is to play on the course and then train specific skills based on how you played. A quick example would be playing 9-holes on the course and learning that putting is your weakness that day. You then go directly to the putting green to train in an effort to improve those skills. Then you get to test how effective your training was the next time you play 9-holes.

Repeat that learning cycle as often as needed to reach your goals. Each time adjusting your training based on the results you are getting on the course.

In some cases that can be a few months or in other cases it could be multiple years, decades or a lifetime as someone prepares to play in high school, college and then in professional golf.

OPERATION 36 LEARNING CYCLE

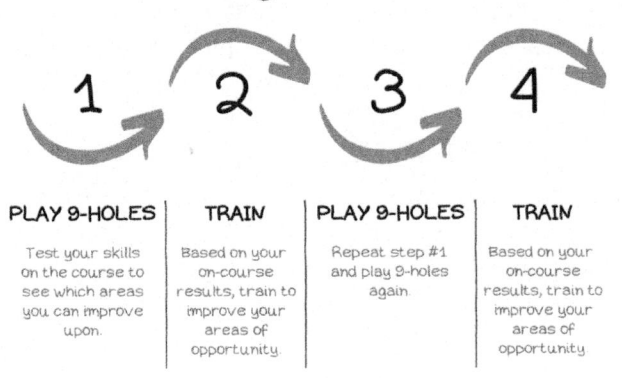

1 → 2 → 3 → 4

PLAY 9-HOLES	TRAIN	PLAY 9-HOLES	TRAIN
Test your skills on the course to see which areas you can improve upon.	Based on your on-course results, train to improve your areas of opportunity.	Repeat step #1 and play 9-holes again.	Based on your on-course results, train to improve your areas of opportunity.

Figure 2: The learning cycle, to us, starts with playing on the course and then is followed up with training. The training is based on the outcomes from playing.

Learning occurs when a player is playing on the golf course and training off the course as long as they are in an environment that provides conditions in which learning is encouraged rather than discouraged.

The Goal

The goal of the Operation 36 Development Model is to "Beat 36" at each level. If you are new to golf, it may be helpful to know that the goal in golf is to use as few golf strokes to get the ball in the hole. As you likely know, the goal is to have the lowest score possible.

We created a Development Model that teaches the appropriate skills and techniques at each phase of learning, or Level. We refer to the Operation 36 Development Model as "scaling by skill." Your playing field (Operation 36 on-course yardage) will adapt as your skill level improves to continue challenging you to get better and better.

Development = Growth

The secret for golfers is to work their way through the model by repetition. In our program, you play golf to get better at golf, something that is typically avoided at all costs in traditional golf programs. **What a shame!**

Here is a few diagrams of the model:

OPERATION 36° GOLF Development Model

STANDARD LEVELS
Level 1
225 Yards
Level 2
450 Yards
Level 3
900 Yards
Level 4
1350 Yards
Level 5
1800 Yards

FULL TEE BOX LEVELS
Level 6
1801-2300 Yards
Level 7
2301-2600 Yards
Level 8
2601-2900 Yards
Level 9
2901-3200 Yards
Level 10
3201+ Yards

Start at 25 yards from the hole and progress back as you improve your skills and beat 36.

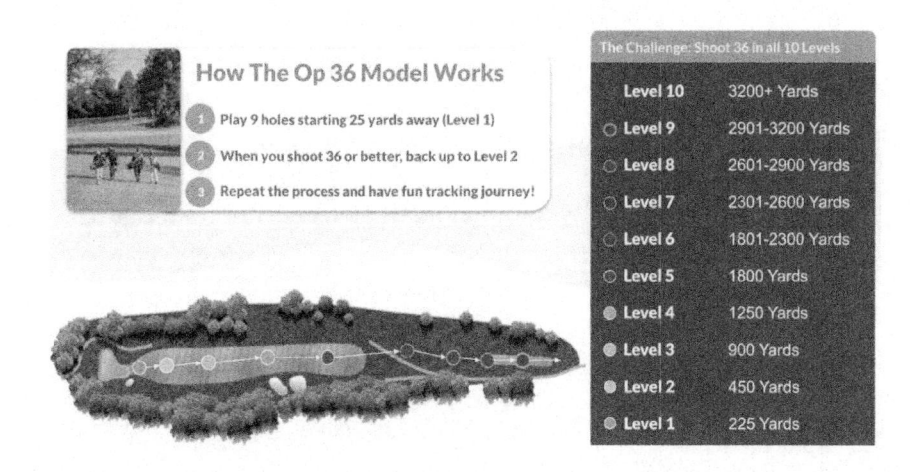

How The Op 36 Model Works

1. Play 9 holes starting 25 yards away (Level 1)
2. When you shoot 36 or better, back up to Level 2
3. Repeat the process and have fun tracking journey!

The Challenge: Shoot 36 in all 10 Levels

Level 10	3200+ Yards
Level 9	2901-3200 Yards
Level 8	2601-2900 Yards
Level 7	2301-2600 Yards
Level 6	1801-2300 Yards
Level 5	1800 Yards
Level 4	1250 Yards
Level 3	900 Yards
Level 2	450 Yards
Level 1	225 Yards

What works so well with this system is that each golfer is always at their perfect challenge point. The golfer is only learning the skills and techniques that are appropriate for their actual ability.

This means that success for each golfer is clearly defined and achievable through hard work and practice. What a tremendous shift this has been for golfers and our industry! Rather than relying on sporadic clinics and clusters of one-on-one coaching, Juniors have a plan to develop as a golfer with developmentally appropriate goals at each step.

The Operation 36 Vision Begins to Spread

As we began to test and improve the Operation 36 Development Model, our classes had grown tremendously, and soon other golf professionals came to us to see what we were doing and to see how they could do it, too. A program we designed to solve our own coaching problems soon began spreading to other golf professionals across the country and abroad.

Soon we made the shift from exclusively helping our own students in a tiny town in North Carolina, to helping thousands of coaches around the world work with tens of thousands of beginner golfers. Our solution spread and, as of this writing, we have nearly 100,000 golfers in our program around the world.

The vision we had to change beginner golf for our students became the catalyst for global change in how the game is taught. Over time our vision was crystalized–Create one million golfers.

In the following chapters, you will find the exact ingredients of this program, and why it is so successful for beginner golfers.

Becoming a Golfer: In their Coaches Words

Cliff Kim – Began Operation 36 at 11 years old
Coach: Dean Kingsbeer, Hutt Valley Golf Course, Moera, Lower Hutt, New Zealand

Cliff Kim started his Operation 36 experience with me at the start of 2016. Cliff was 11 years old and had never played golf before.

After six months of going through the Operation 36 Curriculum, Cliff became skilled enough to advance to the on-course matches I run every other week. In Cliff's first attempt from Level 1 – 25 yards, he scored 41, and was very confident he would pass on his next attempt. He quickly learned how difficult golf is. He patiently went about his play and passed on his fourth try. He passed Level 2 – 50 yards with relative ease, only taking two attempts.

However, Level 3 – 100 yards was a little different. It took Cliff 17 attempts to pass. During this time, I never saw Cliff get upset, angry, or even mention giving up. He continued to work hard on his game. There were, of course, some bad rounds and some close calls, scoring 37 a number of times.

Cliff is now in his fifth year with Operation 36 and continues to go through the ups and downs of this great game. He now plays from Level 6!

I use Cliff's story to help motivate all my players through this amazing junior golf program.

Chapter 4: Finding the Right Level of Challenge

Once we developed a larger Developmental Program, we knew that we had the vision in place for Juniors to be successful. But anyone who has worked with children knows that you have to have more than a plan to keep Juniors engaged.

Overall, the experience needs to be confidence-building and engaging over time. If you have experienced a child dropping out of a sport, it is likely that one of these two needs has not been met.

Let the Environment Work Its Magic

In 1936, Dr. Richard Cabot commissioned a large-scale study to determine if intervening with youths at a young age would prevent or reduce juvenile delinquency. Intervening in this case refers to preventing a student from failing or making a mistake, and in many cases solving the problems for the student. The Cambridge-Somerville Youth Study was composed of 506 boys ages 5-13 who lived in youth facilities in Massachusetts. (Cabot, 1940, 143-151)

The boys in the treatment group were provided a counselor, frequent visits from the counselor, academic tutoring, medical attention, as well as summer camps, Boy Scouts and community programs. The boys in the control group were only asked to report routinely.

Cabot found that initially, and even in a 10 year follow up, the boys in the treatment group who received the interventions did not fare any better than the boys in the control group. While this seems very hard to understand, the interventions did not create a positive outcome for the boys. In some cases, the early intervention led to even more negative results.

As we look at youth sports, and golf in particular, we have also found that interventions tend to work against the golfer. Active, frequent interventions from parents can be disruptive, and not helpful for the child.

In the Operation 36 program, we encourage parents to sit on the sidelines and let the environment (golf course, coach, peer group) work its magic. Yes, we have found that parents try to prevent failures and mistakes, but this is often a missed learning opportunity for the Junior. We recommend that they allow the players to have fun while they are making mistakes, learning and improving. In fact, that is the "secret sauce" of the program, they are having fun while learning to play golf with others.

> "Never solve someone's problem by removing from them the opportunity to solve the problem, that's theft. I'll protect you at the cost of your ability to protect yourself. That destroys people's adaptive competence."
>
> Dr. Jordan B. Peterson

How to Keep Juniors Engaged

Mihaly Csikszentmihalyi is considered to be one of the co-founders of positive psychology. He has spent his career studying happiness, which, to us, is the cousin of the words fun and motivation.

We are **motivated** to pursue things that we **perceive to be fun** because it **makes us happy**!

What Mihaly learned through years of research is that happiness is something we can control with some effort and design. What he found is that people were the most happy when they were in a state that he coined as "Flow."

In his book *Flow: The Psychology of Optimal Experience*, Mihaly defines flow as "when you are so involved in an activity that nothing else seems to matter; people will continue to do it, even at a great cost, for the sheer sake of doing it." (Csikszentmihalyi, 2008, p.4)

The Challenge Point Framework

To put golfers in a "flow state," there is a graph that shows coaches exactly how to do this. It is based on the challenge point framework and was originally created by Mark A. Guadagnoli and Timothy D. Lee. (Guadagnoli & Lee, 2004, 212-224)

The basic thought is that challenges are different for individuals based on their skill level. The coach plays a very important role in tailoring the challenges in hopes of players being in a "flow state" as often as possible.

The job of the coach is to challenge golfers to perform tasks that are just above their current level or ability. We want to put golfers in an environment where they feel they can accomplish the task at hand, but they need to use all the skills they have developed so far to do this. It can't be too hard, and it can't be too easy.

This is the sweet spot! If you can put golfers consistently in the sweet spot, you have the best chance of getting them into a "flow state" and making the golf improvement experience an enjoyable one.

Figure 3: The dotted line represents the challenge point. Where the task/challenge for a player is equal to their skill level.

Over-Challenged State

When we provide our golfers with a task that is too challenging for their skill level, we call this an over-challenged state. This is the worst of the three areas your player can be in, as it creates stress, anxiety, and can evoke very negative emotions.

Figure 4: In this example, the task/challenge is putting the player in a state of anxiousness and frustration. The task/challenge is too difficult for the player's skill level.

When a beginner plays a round of golf from the full tee box, they are often in the Over-Challenged State. Helplessness is a common term for this area. It feels terrible when things are out of your control. Golf loses many beginners because they find themselves in this state.

Under-Challenged State

Now let's take a look at the other side of the spectrum. When you provide an activity or challenge to someone and it is too easy, students will be in a state of boredom. They may do the task, and feel good about themselves for a moment, but will easily be bored and lack engagement or excitement for an activity.

This state is a better place for someone to be in than being over-challenged because they at least feel like they have control of the situation and can achieve what is being presented to them. Sometimes this is a great place to start with someone who is beginning a skill or activity. It helps them to gain confidence and belief that will help them as the challenge increases in difficulty.

Figure 5: In this example, the task/challenge is putting the player in a state of boredom. The task/challenge is too easy for the player's skill level.

The Sweet Spot

As mentioned earlier, the "sweet spot" is where a player is just challenged above their ability. You want whatever activity they are pursuing to seem achievable to them if they worked really hard to do it. This is what puts players in a "flow state."

Finding that sweet spot for golfers on the golf course was the single hardest challenge we faced. We crashed and burned multiple times trying to figure this out. It was pretty easy for us to figure out when we played games on the practice green and driving range, a player's sweet spot. *The golf course was another story...*

Add to it that players are improving their skills over time and the challenge point will move makes this even harder to figure out. It is very easy to under-challenge and over-challenge players.

Discovering the Challenge Point

After the early years of putting players on the tee box and playing scrambles, we knew that wasn't the most effective way to guide players into the game. We did learn one of our greatest lessons when we switched to Operation 36 yardages with our current students.

We hosted a nine-hole event and had all of the golfers begin at 25 yards away in the next 9-hole event. As the players came in after the round you would have thought someone was handing out candy on the course that day! Everyone was smiling, laughing and having a good time.

The common theme was, "Coach, 25 yards was harder than I thought it would be. I did beat 36 and can't wait to try 50 yards next time!"

By the time players got to yardages where they needed 10, 15, 20+ attempts to learn the skills to beat 36, they were mentally and physically ready for the challenge. They had tasted success at 25 yards and 50 yards, they knew they could do it and were willing to put in the work to beat 100 yards.

We nailed it! By using the Challenge Point framework, we had learned to slightly under-challenge players in their first few 9-hole events. The players gained confidence after a handful of attempts, they beat 36 from 25 yards and they were rubbing their hands together to get ready for the next challenge.

And this is how the Operation 36 program is delivered throughout the world now. Everyone starts at a yardage that doesn't overwhelm them, they feel like they can experience success and the student regulates how hard the challenge gets. We use the same Challenge Point framework in the weekly Operation 36 classes, lessons and anytime we are in a learning environment with our students.

> "Practice isn't the thing you do once you're good. It's the thing you do that makes you good."
>
> Malcolm Gladwell
> Author of Outliers

The challenge is that practice is inherently not fun. It's boring and most people try it for the short term and then just quit when they don't see progress. Golf is no different. To stand on a driving range and hit balls for hours upon hours upon hours will drive most to quit before putting in enough time to get to the level of their goals.

Building Confidence while Keeping them Engaged

Over the years, we have learned that allowing the Junior to have some breathing room to try and make mistakes, then learn how to correct them is one of the key ingredients to keeping them interested in the sport over time.

Then presenting them with the right challenge point allows them to continuously improve their skills so that they are happy and engaged in golf for years to come.

Becoming a Golfer: In their Coaches Words

Elizabeth Deckers – Began Operation 36 at 6 Years Old
Coach: Ty Gosnell, PGA – Players Golf Academy, Mount Pleasant, South Carolina

Elizabeth, my first student at Rivertowne C.C. in Charleston, showed up in 2015 at the age of 6. She had never played golf before, but her father thought it might be something that would interest her. For two years, I coached Elizabeth on her swing and fundamentals in weekly lessons. But I never took her on the golf course.

Elizabeth's real golf journey began two years later when I integrated Operation 36 with my program and course play became part of our curriculum. In 2017, Elizabeth shot 47 in her first Operation 36 nine-hole in Level 1 – 25 yards. It took her 12 tries before she passed Level 1 with a score of 33.

In Level 2 – 50 yards, she hit a real challenge point. It took her 20 tries before she shot 35. I frequently coached Elizabeth's parents on patience and expectations when they expressed concern about how long it was taking to get to Level 3. The Operation 36 resources and tools to help parents inspired all four of us to keep pushing through the stacking disappointments.

It was also at this time when Operation 36 started the hashtag #atleast20. Other coaches posted on Instagram using this hashtag and shared stories of players that took at least 20 tournament rounds to pass a challenge point. Elizabeth, her parents, and I openly shared these stories together. The stories significantly helped ease her parents' concerns about Elizabeth's pace. Even better? The #atleast20 stories motivated Elizabeth to stay with golf.

Most players and parents would have stopped or quit playing golf. Most players compare themselves to other players and set unreal expectations. Instead, Elizabeth built a resilient attitude through persistence and is a pillar in our program.

In 2021, we can see her spark. Elizabeth practices harder and more consistently to elevate her game. She is in Level 3 and making strides to prepare for high school golf next year. Watch out, South Carolina!

We are not saying it is not easy, for many this will be the hardest thing they have ever done. What we are saying is that this journey can be fun and we've built fun into every part of the program.

Chapter 5: The Big Picture is Made with Small Steps

As Juniors begin an Operation 36 golf program, they quickly see the bigger picture, and how they can achieve their goal through small, repeated activities.

When a Junior Golfer plays nine holes from Level 1 - 25 yards away, they get to experience success. Once a player plays a round and is around others on the same journey, they begin their golf journey with a positive experience. We start with progression, not regression.

Some golfers get their first par, birdie or even hole-in-one in the first round they ever played! They may not beat 36 in their first attempt but they are so excited to play again as they tasted some success and can see with some practice that they can move on to Level 2 - 50 yards! The app, coach, friends, and model then encourage the player to try to beat their score by one stroke the next time they play.

Since the Junior feels like this is achievable, they are motivated to work on their game to try to achieve this goal. This starts the cycle of wanting to play and practice golf. They have the big picture, vision and plan of them going from their first round to shooting par from a full tee box. The destination is set, it is time to embark on the journey!

With the vision ahead of us, next we look at the day-to-day training on a micro scale to develop the Junior golfer. This includes the education and day-to-day training activities in classes. Like adults, Juniors also want to be in an environment where they can make their own choices, develop skills, and fit in with others in a group setting.

This is why we recommend having group classes where golfers will not only train their skills using games, but also work through a six-level educational curriculum that helps empower them with education. Golfers in the program know they are going to learn new skills as they progress and have a coach to guide them so they never feel lost.

Curriculum

Could you imagine enrolling your child in a school without a curriculum? No written plan? No grades? That is hard for many of us to consider! We think that youth athletics should be held to the same standard for development.

After being in the golf coaching profession for many years, we can confidently say that the lack of structure and curriculum for instruction is the reason that only 1.6 out of every 100 beginners actually becomes a golfer! Many coaches are very busy and create their lesson plans (especially in the early years) at the last minute.

Does Karate have a set training program or curriculum? Yes, they have learned that having a belt system with defined skills that are learned in class and tested every 60 days is a recipe for long term success.

Go into any Karate Dojo and you will see students that have been in the program for many years as they work through the curriculum to improve. The curriculum is what helps them along the journey to see small wins along the way as they work toward their ultimate goal of achieving a Black Belt.

Does Gymnastics have a set training program or curriculum? Yes, they have defined this for the gymnasts as Level 1 - Level 10. It is simple for the athlete to know where they are and what skills they need to work on to achieve their goals. If a gymnast wants to be in the Olympics someday, they know they need to get to Level 10.

Go into any Gymnastics facility and you will see students that have been in the program for many years. They understand that to improve they need to put in the time and effort to develop the skills to reach their goals. The curriculum helps the student to see progress as they build skill after skill to ultimately reach their long term goals.

Why not Golf?

The Operation 36 Curriculum

By observing players over the years, we have noticed some common skills or fundamentals that every player needs to develop to beat 36 at each level on the course.

These common skills were put into a six-level curriculum in 2014 and then refined over and over again over the years as players and coaches around the world used them and provided feedback. This curriculum is used by the majority of Operation 36 programs around the world to help guide players to developing the skills needed to progress. As of the writing of this book we are on version 9.3 of the curriculum. The six-level curriculum has 12 skills in each level that a player can learn as they advance.

Similar to the school system, our six levels can be viewed as grades (or belts, if you are familiar with the martial arts). Every player in Operation 36 starts in Level 1 – Orange and can advance all the way to Rank 6 – Black.

- Level 1 – Orange
- Level 2 – Yellow
- Level 3 – Green
- Level 4 – Blue
- Level 5 – Purple
- Level 6 – Black

As of the writing of this book, coaches around the world have the choice in delivering the curriculum.

1. **Traditional format** - To advance through a Level, a player must earn all 12 skills. Once all 12 skills have been earned through testing, they unlock the next set of 12 skills. This is similar to Karate.
2. **Performance format** - To advance through a Level, a player must beat 36 from the on-course yardage in a 9-hole event. For example, a player beats 36 from Level 1 - 25 yards, they advance immediately to Level 2 - 50 yards and unlock the next 12 skills. In this case, the coach defines success as performing on the course. The strategy is that if they can perform on the course and beat 36, they have demonstrated the skill and can move to the next level.

Both formats have proven to be very effective in delivery and we leave it to each Coach to determine the best fit for their facility and coaching style.

Each skill can be viewed like a subject in school. For example, in school we have math, science, history and English. In Operation 36, we have Putting, Power, Posture and Ball Flight.

Each one of the 12 skills has two parts:

1. **Cognitive Understanding** – A player needs to acquire the knowledge and understanding of the skill.
2. **Demonstration** – A player then needs to be able to demonstrate proficiencty that is appropriate for that particular level.

At each Level, the curriculum spells out the skills needed to beat 36 at each yardage on the course with the same Level in the curriculum. This helps to bring the essential *purpose* of the curriculum, and how it can help the golfer at the nine-hole events.

As of the writing of this book, these are the 12 skills in the curriculum. The name of the skills stay the same at all 6 levels.

However, the skills increase at each level in detail and challenge to help a player beat 36 at each yardage.

For example, Level 1 – Grip and Level 4 – Grip are very different. They may be the same subject, but the detail and challenge are very different as someone who needs to beat 36 from Level 1 - 25 yards only needs a very basic understanding of the grip and someone who is trying to beat 36 from Level 4 - 150 yards, might need the final details added to help them hit the ball consistently solid, far and straight.

As an example:

Level 1 Grip - Lock and Cover

A coach might share the general concepts of where the left hand and right hand should be on the grip. The left hand is positioned where the grip is locked under the heel pad of the left hand for leverage and control. The right hand then covers the left thumb. This would give a player a great start to the game and allow a coach to add more detail to each hand and finger later.

Level 4 Grip - Trigger Finger

At Level 4 a coach is filling in the details to the player on exactly where the right forefinger (right handed golfer) is located both on the grip and in relation to the other fingers. This is a very detailed piece of the grip and a coach will go over how for a normal full swing shot, a player wants the forefinger to be on the side of the grip. Many times players will rotate the forefinger too far to the right or left which can result in shots that go offline. This also opens up a conversation on the hand, forearm, elbow and shoulder and where that is placed can effect the trigger finger as well.

1. Technical Skills
   a. Putting - Learn how to use the putter efficiently to get the ball into the hole.
   b. Power - Learn how to hit the golf ball far distances.
   c. Posture - Learn how to maintain your posture for consistent, powerful golf swings.
   d. Grip - Learn how to grip the club to swing it effectively.
   e. Alignment - Learn how to align your target and influence different ball flights.
   f. Ball Flight - Learn how to execute different shots and control the club face and path.
   g. Green Reading - Learn how to predict how the ball will roll on the green when putting.

2. Knowledge Skills
   a. Mastery - Learn information that will help you master golf.
   b. Honor - Learn rules, history of golf, and how to play the game.
   c. Fitness -Learn how to prepare and take care of your body to perform at your best.

3. Reps and On-Course
   a. Work Ethic - Golfers achieve milestones when they log playing and training in the Op 36 App.
   b. Performance - Golfers achieve milestones as they play golf and shoot 36 or better in a division.

Repetition in Learning

We have learned over the years how important repetition is in learning a skill. Instead of repetition, we like to use the word spacing. We were introduced to the concept of spacing by Iain Highfield, from his book 'Golf Practice: How to Practice Golf and Take Your Range Game to the Course.' It is defined as the amount of time between learning a skill and reviewing or practicing it again. (Highfield, 2019)

It is unfair for coaches to expect a player to remember something that was only taught to them one time. We are humans, therefore, we typically forget that information.

All of us experience the "forgetting curve." Researchers say that within an hour of learning something, we forget 50% of what was taught. Within 24 hours, we forget 70% of the information. (Ruger & Bussenius, 1913)

How can we expect players to learn something they were only exposed to once? For the Junior to be successful, we need to create a learning system where they can review what they learned at any time and where we as coaches can direct them to go to learn outside of our in-person lessons for reinforcement.

The Mobile App is Born

As we were coaching golf with this curriculum, we were frustrated because we knew they needed a workbook to help them reinforce the ideas learned in class.

If you have worked with children, you know how hard it can be to get them to remember to bring a workbook each week to their lesson. So we created a mobile app that would track the progress of the golfer, while allowing them to practice and review new concepts covered in their golf lesson each week.

When a student learned a new skill or completed a milestone, there would be automated celebrations in the app. When a coach marks a skill complete from the curriculum on their phone, the player and parent automatically gets a notification confirming it.

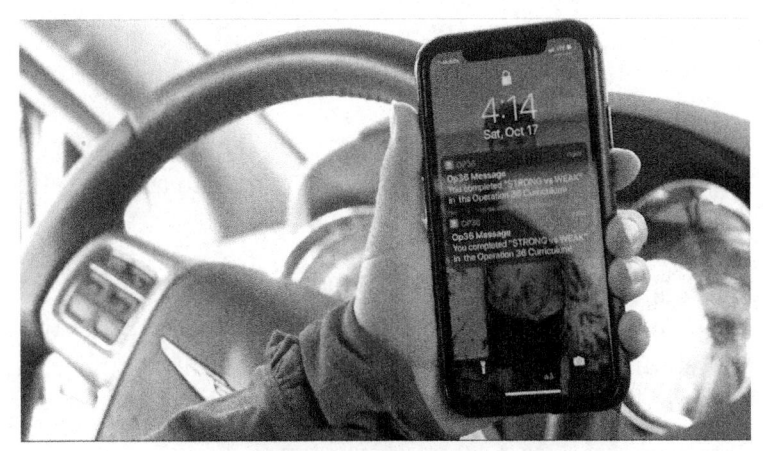

A parent receives a notification that their child earned a new skill while they are waiting in the car.

It has made a huge difference in motivation and showing students progress right after they completed something.

In the Operation 36 program, a coach will create a schedule of events for the semester or year in the app for the player, parent and coach to reference at all times. A player knows ahead of time which of the 12 skills are covered and can watch the curriculum video on a mobile device prior to arriving to class to be aware of what will be covered.

After class and the weeks following, they can watch it again to catch anything they may have missed. When a coach runs a testing week to verify the skills have been learned, a player can watch the videos once again to help prepare them for the test. It's a great learning tool and is available to all Operation 36 participants around the world.

The Curriculum is Ever-Evolving

At the time of this writing, we are working on new updates to the curriculum. We use the feedback from coaches and families to see how we can improve and make the experience even more impactful. But we have found that the standardization of the skills has made all the difference in the beginner golfer experience.

Becoming a Golfer: In their Coaches Words

Harry Nudson – Began Operation 36 at 5 Years Old
Coach: Jake Martin, PGA – Louisville, Kentucky

Harry's grandfather is a member at our club, and he heard the professional staff talking about Operation 36 in March of 2018. He mentioned his grandson was interested in learning and would like to be a part of this new program. This was our first session utilizing the Operation 36 platform at the club, and I needed as many juniors as I could to show how amazing our program could be, so I told his grandfather we would love to have him as part of our group.

Harry, at the time, was just 5 years old! From day one, you could tell Harry was in it for the long haul. While he was very young, he immediately started in with our private individual lessons in addition to the Operation 36 curriculum.

Harry's first round from Level 1 – 25 yards finished with a score of 63, and he had 43 putts to achieve that score. He left the scoreboard with a huge smile and had officially bought in! His youth was a factor for sure in his "struggles" from 25 yards, but he continued to work through the program! Harry passed Level 1 – 25 yards on his 12th attempt with a score of 35 and a total of 18 putts! I sat with him afterwards and chatted about his accomplishment. I let him know how proud I was of his efforts and hard work. We also talked about how the next yardage will provide a whole new set of challenges for him. He said, "I am in, coach!"

Harry started Level 2 – 50 yards the following spring and worked hard to pass. He was taking lessons from our staff and working on the course with his dad. I would see his postings on the Operation

36 feed taking the Golf at Home Challenge, hitting balls at home, playing courses and putting! Harry has not quite passed 50 yards yet. His baseline score is 53 with 38 putts. But his lowest score so far is a 38 with 19 putts!

To say Harry is excited to succeed would be a huge understatement. He continues to take lessons and practice. His family has officially joined the club, so he has unlimited access to achieve his goals and is, "still in, coach!" I will watch this young man when he doesn't think I am, and I still see the IYAL with toe tap (opening skill that all students learn) and the occasional fist pump! I see Harry at the practice green working on his distance control and reading greens.

Watching Harry grow over the past three and a half years has been amazing, and he exemplifies what we are trying to accomplish at our club with the Operation 36 program!

Chapter 6: The "Secret Sauce" to Keeping Your Junior Golfer Motivated

Despite what you may have thought, you don't have to be a great golfer to have a lot of fun with golf! Juniors will stay in the game as long as they are having a good time and they are motivated to achieve their next goal.

When Juniors understand "why" they are doing a particular activity, they are often much more engaged. In fact, we would call it an essential ingredient. Understanding the "why" behind different activities and drills keeps a player's internal motivation strong. It is especially important when a golfer hits some "bumps in the road" or has the inevitable day or week that they are down and want to quit golf.

Our original students from 2011 to 2014 had a blast coming to the course everyday to play games and have fun at the training facility. However, they got to a point where they didn't understand what they were working towards each week. They didn't have a clearly defined goal for the future. Eventually they grew out of the games after a few years and we didn't have the next step ready for them.

In baseball, basketball, soccer, ice hockey and every other sport, your training leads to playing a game. During an actual game, the player has a lot of fun and learns the "why" behind their practice. An athlete typically has some good plays in the game, and they also notice where they need to improve. That's how they learn, improve, and are motivated to play more.

Here are some common things we hear from youth players we've coached in our town recreational league baseball, softball, basketball and soccer teams:

"Coach, why do we have to practice so much, I just want to play in the game?"

"Coach, I can't wait for the game this weekend!"

"Coach, we are playing against my friend Tom in the next game. I want to work hard in practice to be able to compete with him."

"Coach, in the game last night, I had trouble hitting, can we work on hitting in practice tonight?"

We have NEVER heard these comments from youth players:

"Coach, I just want to do the throwing and catching we do at every practice."

"Coach, can I just come to the practices and field ground balls? I don't want to play in the game."

"Coach, can I sit on the bench today for the game? I only like practice."

"Coach, I don't want a uniform and feel like part of the team. I only come for the practices."

The fun part of sports is the actual Game! You will hear this point over and over again in this book, playing the game of golf on the golf course is fun for all ages and abilities when experienced from the appropriate yardage based on skill.

Most Effective Motivation

The most effective form of motivation is progress, no matter how small it is. (Clear, 2018) As humans, we crave progress in everything we do.

Ask anyone who is training to complete a 5K race if progress is important to them. The ones we have met keep track of the pace of every mile they run in training. They try to find every little advantage to improve. Whether this is the perfect shoe or the best pre-race snack, most runners are looking for any advantage! For those that have run for quite some time, the goal turns from just finishing the race to improving their time in the next one.

And for Juniors, they are also motivated by progress. It is common to see a child start a Lego project and be so focused on finishing it that they disregard everything else for hours on end. Take a 7 year old to the park and it's not enough to hang from the first monkey bar. The child quickly wants to move to the second monkey bar, then the third and then finally to finish it.

How about a 10 year old that opens the most popular video game of all time, that has sold over 238 million copies to date: Minecraft. Its popularity is due to the user's ability to progress in gathering things and creating things. They want to make progress in the game.

When we do something and see progress, it motivates us internally to want to get even better. A key ingredient to its effectiveness in motivating us is that this progress needs to be acknowledged and seen by the participant as soon as possible. This is important for adults and especially with children – they need to see some progress or they get frustrated and give up.

We made a very big mistake early on when we were coaching. Players would make progress in class or on the golf course and we didn't celebrate it or show them. We didn't know how important that celebrating progress was at the time. More importantly, we had no way to easily pull the data to be able to know when they were making progress.

At that time, we tracked everything on a paper spreadsheet, and with 80 students it was nearly impossible to be up to date on each player's history. Paper would be lost, damaged in the weather, or binders would be left at home. These players missed out on a huge opportunity to gain motivation and it was certainly our fault.

That has changed now with the use of the Operation 36 Mobile App. Coaches now have on-demand data and we can access it real time by pulling out our phone.

It is common to see a coach, at the end of a nine-hole event round, pull his phone or tablet out to see within seconds to check on a player's personal best score (lowest score to date). When a player approaches the scoring table, the coach knows if they can celebrate a personal best or milestone completed and see a player's entire journey at a click of a button.

Lee Sunggeon, Op 36 certified coach, with a student who just beat 36 and advanced to the next level.

If you don't play the game of golf on a consistent basis, you will not show progress on the course and will lose motivation to play the game.

We saw it in our first 40 players we lost and we see it to this day in players that just play games and do drills on the practice area. Yes, it is fun for the short term, but over time it gets old if a player doesn't understand the purpose and see progress.

It breaks our heart to see a Dad teaching a 7 year old on the driving range to keep their "head down." Ball after ball, the Dad corrects the 7 year old on their technique. The story ends almost the same with the child turning to Dad and saying, "I don't want to do this anymore."

Alternatively, we jump for joy (and the parents do as well) when a beginner player is introduced to the game by playing in an Operation 36 nine-hole event. They come off the course beaming with excitement and can't wait for the next opportunity to play. More often than not, they have met some new friends, had some good holes, and are curious on what they can work on to be better next time. Now that is a winning formula!

To best understand where you or your players interest is, get with your local Operation 36 coach to get some guidance on what option is available at your facility and which one is best for you.

Consistent Playing Helps the Coach

Without playing consistently, a coach is guessing as to where to prioritize what to focus on to help a Junior in class or a lesson. Should we work on your full swing woods, irons or wedges? Is it your chipping, pitching or bunker shots that needs to improve? Is it your long putts? Short putts?

Ask any Coach whose players don't play on the course regularly if they are guessing on where to help their players to see the most improvement in their on course skills. They would be lying if they didn't say "yes."

Inevitably, if a coach can't see what they are doing on the course, they default to working on a player's golf swing. That's how we were trained as golf professionals. Is that the most effective area to work on to help them progress on the course? More often than not for beginner golfers, it is not.

Contrast that with a Coach that has a player that plays on a consistent basis and the scores/stats are logged in the Operation 36 Mobile App to reference. The beginning of a lesson is much different.

Here is a typical conversation in that situation:

Op36 Coach: "After seeing your progression in the app, you are improving. You've lost 3 strokes in the last month."

Student: "Really? I didn't realize that. I was getting a little frustrated that I wasn't improving."

Op36 Coach: "Yeah, it is showing your personal best is now a 39 at Level 3 – 100 yards and you are three strokes away from beating 36."

Student: "Oh. What do I need to do better to beat 36?"

Op36 Coach: "It looks like you are hitting plenty of greens as you are averaging seven, so the work we've been doing on your swing and course management has been working very well. The next area to focus on is your chipping and putting as your average putts per nine holes is 17.4, and our goal to beat 36 will require 15 putts or less."

Student: "Oh, ok, let's work on my chipping and putting today.

If your Junior is playing consistently and your coach can see the scores and basic stats, they will know what area to focus on to improve. Then you will spend your time wisely in lessons and in your training. This is a long-term recipe for improving at the fastest rate and reducing the frustration of not seeing improvement.

The time it takes someone to complete an activity, receive feedback, and then work to improve the skill is a critical part of the development process. If it takes too long, the likelihood to take action decreases with every minute, hour, and day. You may have heard of this loop – it is referred to as the feedback loop.

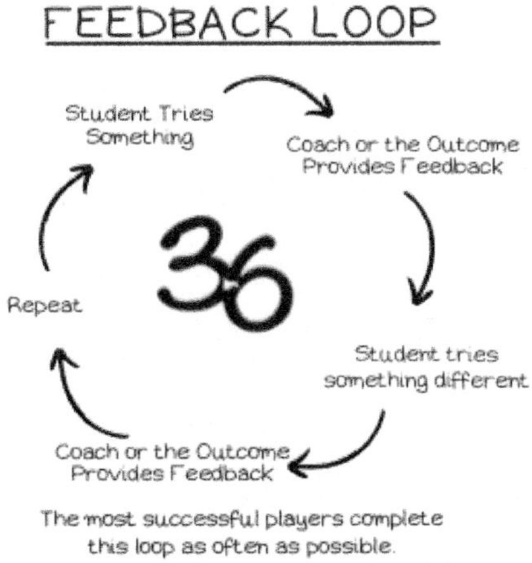

FEEDBACK LOOP

Student Tries Something → Coach or the Outcome Provides Feedback → Student tries something different → Coach or the Outcome Provides Feedback → Repeat

36

The most successful players complete this loop as often as possible.

Figure 6: In an Operation 36 nine-hole event, class or training a student starts by trying something. The coach and/or the outcome provide feedback. The student then tries something different and evaluates the outcome.

"I think it's very important to have a feedback loop, where you're constantly thinking about what you've done and how you could be doing it better. I think that's the single best piece of advice -- constantly think about how you could be doing things better and questioning yourself."
    - Elon Musk, Founder of Tesla and SpaceX

The goal is to shorten the feedback loop as much as possible and repeat the entire process as many times as possible. The players that improve the most and reach the highest level in any activity and sport do this. As you will learn in later chapters, we need to honor the development of each player and not push them into more competition than they are emotionally and physically ready for. However, when the time is right and they want to play more, we need to be ready to support them.

Did Tiger Woods play one junior tournament a year when he was 14 years old? No. His father knew the power of repetition from his military training, and Tiger played a lot. He didn't win every tournament, as no one does, but he did learn from each event to help him improve, and eventually all those feedback loops he completed led to him being one of the greatest players of all time.

A simple example would be a player who finishes his round and doesn't get a chance to take action for seven days. Another player who finished playing immediately learned what they needed to improve and then took action right away by going to the putting green to train. The player who immediately went to the putting green to train has an advantage over the player who won't get a chance to train for seven days.

Many times Juniors want to stay after the round to work on putting or hitting some balls on the range to practice something they saw that needed improvement during the class, which is fantastic! Our goal is to get feedback to our players as fast as possible so they can get back to training as fast as possible.

Purposeful and Informed

For a golfer's training to have the greatest possible impact, the training must be purposeful and informed. If there is an area of the game that needs improvement but they work on another area, it won't help the weaknesses improve. It seems crazy that we need to state that in this book, yet hours upon hours of training each year is done by players that aren't engaging in purposeful and informed training.

The Operation 36 Mobile App does a great job of looking at how you create your score (see next section on 6:15 stats) and delivers purposeful and informed games and training activities for your Junior to perform right after you finish your round – purposeful activities delivered immediately after they play.

In addition, your Junior's coach can see the results of their training in the app and can alter their recommendations to your Junior based on this. This is truly an amazing feedback loop if you think about it and one that can help someone reach their potential the fastest with the least amount of time wasted. When your Junior understands the greater picture, and why they are working on specific activities, they will be motivated to give their best effort and to continue, even when times are tough.

Becoming a Golfer: In their Coaches Words

Calvin Scott – Began Operation 36 at 7 Years Old
Coach: Jameson Wallace – Chambersburg C.C., Chambersburg, Pennsylvania

Calvin joined our academy in the spring of 2017 as one of the original five students in our academy. The then-7-year-old may have lacked size (he was 45 inches tall at the time) but he certainly did not lack a passion for the game, as evidenced throughout his journey by his extreme passion for golf, the program, and our academy. His on-course journey began with success as he passed the first three levels of Operation 36 within five attempts at his young age.

The journey was not always so easy. Flash forward two years, and Calvin reached his challenge point at Level 5 – 200 yards. What seemed like a natural evolution of on-course progress hit a wall. He didn't waver, give up or spend any less time and effort on improving his game. Thirty-four attempts later, he was successful on an April day, two years after his initial enrollment in the program.

What is not most impressive about Calvin and his journey is not his on course success, not his fame earned through his national finalist status in the Drive, Chip & Putt with a trip to Augusta National for the Masters and significant television coverage on the Golf Channel, but his attitude.

Throughout his development, Calvin has been a cheerleader for the program, with complete buy-in to everything we've asked. He was always an active participant in class, bringing friends every chance he could, coming prepared for testing, and even encouraging and caddie for his younger siblings as they picked up the game. His love for the program was even recognized as another local club asked an 11-year-old Calvin to assist in coaching their junior golf camp.

Calvin is now a standard-bearer for our academy, showing what can be accomplished and demonstrating how juniors should conduct themselves in achieving our mission to create long-term golfers.

Chapter 7: Why this System Works

Over the years, the Operation 36 Program has become the fastest growing golf program in the world. This isn't just because we play golf backwards or have a framework and technology to support each golfer's development.

Under the program, there are a couple pillars in our program that have been pivotal in its sustained long term success. The first is that we have a tool to help coaches, players and parents to know exactly what the golfer needs to focus on next. This is our signature, "6:15 Stat System."

The second is that throughout our program, the focus is on getting the golfer onto the golf course frequently with 9-hole events, where the 6:15 Stat System is utilized. These 9-hole events allow the golfer to fall in love with playing golf, and help them to see the purpose of why they practice each week with their coach.

Why Play in Formal Nine-Hole Events?

When it comes time to test your Junior's skills, competing against themselves in a formal environment has proven to be the most effective. In an environment where everyone is competing against the course with a common goal of shooting 36 or better, players are supporting each other and everyone wants to improve. Juniors want to see the other players do well, they also want others to support them!

It is commonplace to see players in an Operation 36 program training together on the range and the course outside of formal programming. These same players develop strong friendships that lead to participation in other events both at the golf course and in the community.

Everyone has different goals and motivation in playing the game of golf. And as you will learn, goals and motivation change as a player moves through different phases of life. Some adults want to get good enough to be comfortable playing with friends, in the local charity four-person scrambles, or in local amateur events. Some Juniors want to improve enough to play on their middle school or high school team, in college and beyond.

In any case, learning the skill of performing in a formal event is one that a player should be exposed to at the right time. It's a different environment than playing casually with friends and family, where you can possibly drop a second ball to try again or possibly not even keep score. And if you speak to players, it is a much more rewarding experience when you've worked hard for something and do it in front of your peers or others.

Playing in the nine-hole events and demonstrating the ability to shoot 36 or better is a much more effective experience to prepare someone to play in the above mentioned goals. It is commonplace to hear a participant in Operation 36 say after playing in the nine-hole events for a period of time that it prepared them for success in other events.

Finally, it reduces the likelihood of false scores. Casually playing with family and friends provides the opportunity to skate the rules. Playing in a formal nine-hole event put on by your coach at your course has systems in place to greatly reduce this.

The beauty of the Operation 36 levels on the course is that it makes it more accessible for families to play golf together on the course. Everyone has their own yardage that is skill appropriate and enjoyable. Everyone can play at a good pace, and you could even have a friendly competition against each other. What kid doesn't want to beat their Dad?

It is common at our facilities in the late afternoon and evenings to see a Junior Golfer on the course playing from 50 yards, Mom at 150 yards and Dad at the white tees. We hear from other Operation 36 coaches around the world that they are seeing the same thing on a regular basis at their facility. The culture in golf is changing!

The 6:15 Stat System

The best players in the world use very detailed stat systems to find out exactly where they can improve from year to year. Often, they are looking to get .25 to .5 strokes better per round from year to year. To find these fractions of strokes, and to make sure they aren't going to get worse in other categories, they employ full-time statisticians to help them analyze this data.

After analyzing this data, they meet with their team of swing coaches, fitness trainers, short game specialists and training program coordinators to develop specific practice programs. The real challenge lies in maintaining all of your skills while improving in certain areas of focus. It's not easy!

The Operation 36 program uses a system that simplifies exactly what the golfer needs to focus on next to improve. We call it the "6:15 Stat System" and it is one that allows coaches to quickly identify the weaknesses in the player's game. Rest assured, you don't need a full time statistician or team of coaches to use this system.

This simple and highly effective system provides informed feedback with actionable information within seconds of finishing a round. It is not the most complex statistical tracking system in the golf industry. But we are a program designed for beginners, not Tour players!

The goal is to hit six or more greens and have 15 or less putts. We have learned that if a player does meet these two statistical categories they have a very high likelihood of beating 36.

Greens in Regulation (GIR)

A player must stop their ball on the putting green in two or less strokes per hole in Operation 36 to qualify as a green in regulation, or GIR. The goal for a nine-hole course is to hit at least 6 greens. If it takes a player more than 2 strokes, it does not count as a GIR.

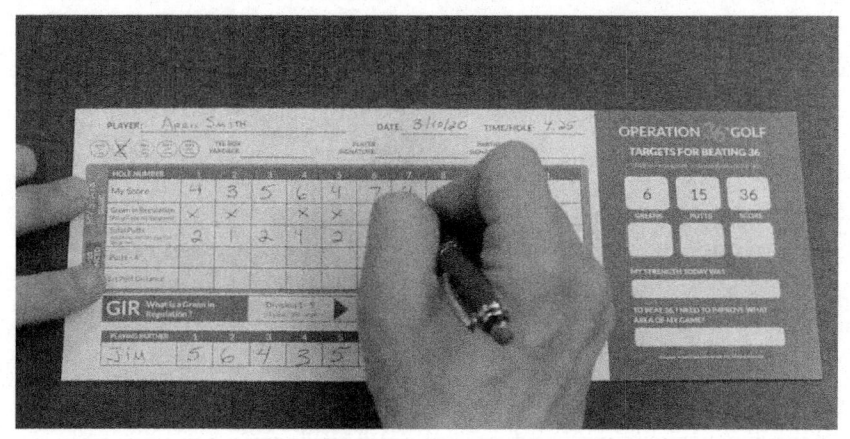

A student completing an Operation 36 Scorecard that utilizes the 6:15 Stat System.

Using the Operation 36 scorecards, a player simply checks or puts an 'X' in the GIR row after each hole. For younger players, a parent or caddie can do this. At the end of the round they add up the row and can compare that to the standard of six.

If they had less than six, this gives the player and coach a great place to start to figure out how to improve. They can work together to answer the question, "How do I stop the ball on the green in two shots or less more often?"

Total Putts

The other important stat is total putts. We define a putt as a shot played from on the putting green. The goal is to have 15 or less putts for 9 holes.

At the end, the Junior adds them up and compares that to the standard of 15. If they have more than 15 putts, they can work with their coach on precisely what skill needs to be improved in their short game to improve this stat next time.

Again, the speed at which someone gets the feedback is very important. 6:15 is not the most complex stat tracking system available. However, for the purposes of Operation 36, it is the perfect blend of speed and accuracy.

Timely Feedback

The 6:15 Stat System, utilized in routine 9-hole events, provides clear, routine feedback for the Junior Golfer, coach and family. This is the most expedient way to provide that specific feedback so that the golfer and coach know fully what needs to be practiced to improve and beat 36.

It is common after a nine-hole event for a player to learn they didn't hit enough greens or had too many putts and immediately ask Mom or Dad to go to the practice facility. What a great learning environment! The player is motivated to work on their game right after playing. That is a recipe for long term success!

Becoming a Golfer: Stories from Operation 36 Coaches

Adalyn Murphy – Began Operation 36 at 14 Years Old
Coach: Ryne Burnett, PGA – Kenwood C.C., Cincinnati, Ohio

Nearly every adult that passes me and says a kind word about our Junior academy says they wish they would have started to play golf at a younger age using the Operation 36 Junior Golf Development Model. I imagine they would feel differently if they were a young lady just starting high school, never having played a round of golf before. The social ramifications of even thinking of trying something new or different is scary enough before beginning to embrace the challenging journey to becoming a golfer.

This golfer joined our Operation 36 program in the spring of 2021. We squeezed her into a group with a few other young ladies in a regular academy class, since she was the only player registered for the 13 to 17 girls only group. In the spring nine-hole events, her three attempts at Level 1 – 25 yards averaged just over 40 shots, with 28 putts averaged per round. You could tell she was not keen on trying the events anymore. She was so close, but not achieving success, and did not want to experience disappointment yet again, but thankfully, we tried again in the next session.

I explained to her that the way to finally breaking 36 was through putting. If she closed the gap from 28 to 15 putts in half, that is an easy seven or eight stroke improvement on her score. A few weeks before the next event, I noticed her at the club more and more with her family, and she was spending time at the short game area. Her practice paid off, and in her fourth attempt, she only had 16 total putts, a 12-stroke improvement. She only hit the ball 10 other times, resulting in a score of 26 from 25 yards! Not only was the score the lowest out over 350 rounds played in 2021 events, she iced the cake when she turned in her scorecard, and said, "I swear, I didn't cheat!"

The point of her story is not that she shot an incredible 26 from nine holes (one shot off a three-year standing course record). This young lady decided to improve where she needed to improve in order to accomplish her goal, instead of shying away after three failed attempts. She chose to embrace the opportunity to improve outside of her comfort zone, and be rewarded for the efforts she made, which will pay dividends for her as she continues to grow as a person. She is now working at Level 2, 50 yards, and will be taking private lessons this winter so she is ready to go for 2022 and the rest of her life.

Chapter 8: How to Properly Develop a Junior Athlete

When Juniors fall in love with golf, and are interested in progressing in the sport, many parents are not quite sure how to help them continue to improve.

Every sport needs a path from beginner to mastery or the highest level. You see this in other sports, like the progression from pee-wee football, to a high school team, NCAA then to the NFL. Each sport must have a path forward that develops the athlete to progress to the next step.

We were exposed to Long Term Athlete Development (or LTAD) for golf through educational seminars by the Titleist Performance Institute back in the early 2000s. More specifically, it was the modern day work of Istvan Balyi that was shared in those seminars and made public by the Canadian government through open source documents. (Balyi, 2019)

The LTAD and Balyi's work helped to uncover what needs to be done at each stage of human development to give every child the best chance of engaging in lifelong, health-enhancing physical activity. Further, for those with drive and talent, what needs to be accomplished at each development stage to ensure the best chance of athletic success.

The widespread interest in the LTAD model was prompted by a poor finish in the 2004 Olympics by the Canadians, which was attributed to a decaying national sports system. (Eisenmann, 2018) At the same time, Balyi began consulting with national sporting organizations in England, Ireland, Australia, New Zealand and elsewhere.

Thus, we can certainly give thanks to Canada for its contribution to the modern-day LTAD that is used by so many countries and organizations throughout the world.

Long-Term Development in Sport and Physical Activity

Sport for Life

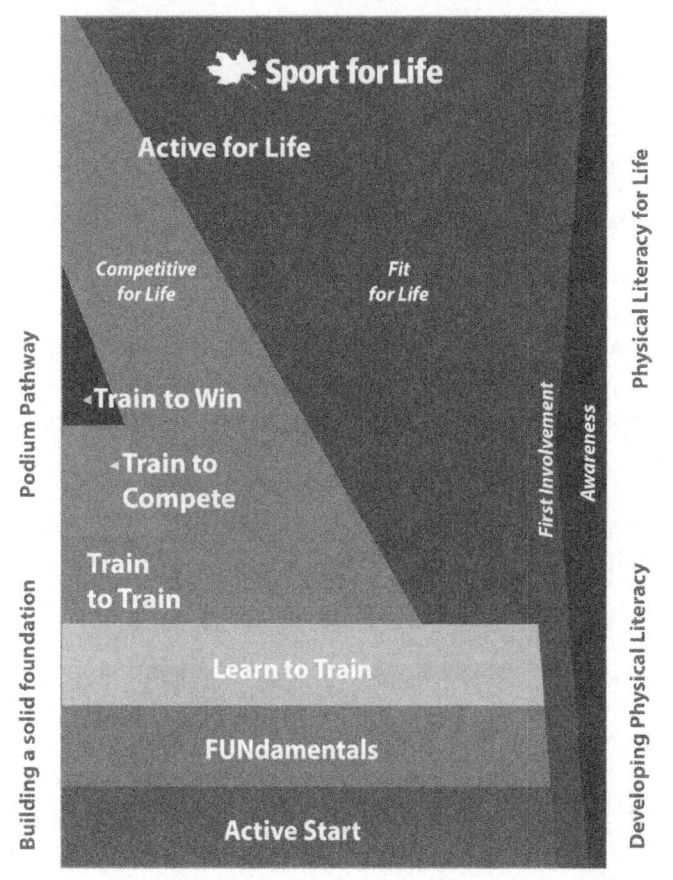

- Active for Life
- Competitive for Life
- Fit for Life
- ◂Train to Win
- ◂Train to Compete
- Train to Train
- Learn to Train
- FUNdamentals
- Active Start

Podium Pathway — Building a solid foundation

First Involvement — Awareness

Physical Literacy for Life — Developing Physical Literacy

Figure 7: The seven-stage LTAD model shows a citizen's age from bottom to top. Thus, an infant would start in the Active Start phase, go through Fundamentals and would end up at the top of the chart, Fit for Life. Each phase has guidelines specific to the age of the citizen for everyone to be aware of or as is commonly stated, "Doing the right thing at the right time." From *Canadian Sport For Life.*

To support the delivery of the seven-stage LTAD model are key factors which are represented in an age- and developmentally-appropriate manner within each stage.

It has taken a while for the U.S. to adopt LTAD for a variety of reasons. The lightning strike to get American governing bodies moving may have been seeing the success of Canada at the Olympics, or possibly the decline in youth sport participation in the U.S. that eventually led to the tipping point.

In 2014, the U.S. Olympic and Paralympic Committee adapted and adopted ADM (American Development Model) for a multitude of sports. The governing bodies in golf (LPGA Tour, PGA Tour, Augusta National, USGA) followed suit in 2019 with adapting the ADM for golf.

Prior to 2019, Operation 36 had been pioneering a way to guide a beginner golfer and provide him or her with a clear, encouraging path to become a life-long golfer. We combined everything that we learned about athlete and player development into a system that would be fun for a Junior golfer, and keep them engaged for the long-term.

Operation 36 Junior Golf Development Model

In our view, too many programs never take the "time outs" needed at certain times of a player's development to evaluate, see what is working, and make adjustments. They just keep plugging along, year after year and sometimes miss these crucial opportunities to make adjustments that will have negative and sometimes permanent effects.

The Junior Golf Development Model allows us to take a time out and see if what we are doing is working based on years and years of data on thousands upon thousands of players using the same standardized on-course development model.

The Purpose of the Development Model

Parents and coaches should have a clear golf development model to know exactly where the Junior is in their golf skill development and how to play a positive role every step of the way.

The Junior Golf Development Model allows the player, parent, and coach to make adjustments and tweaks along the way to maximize the golf skill training and develop the healthiest mindset for someone to reach their potential.

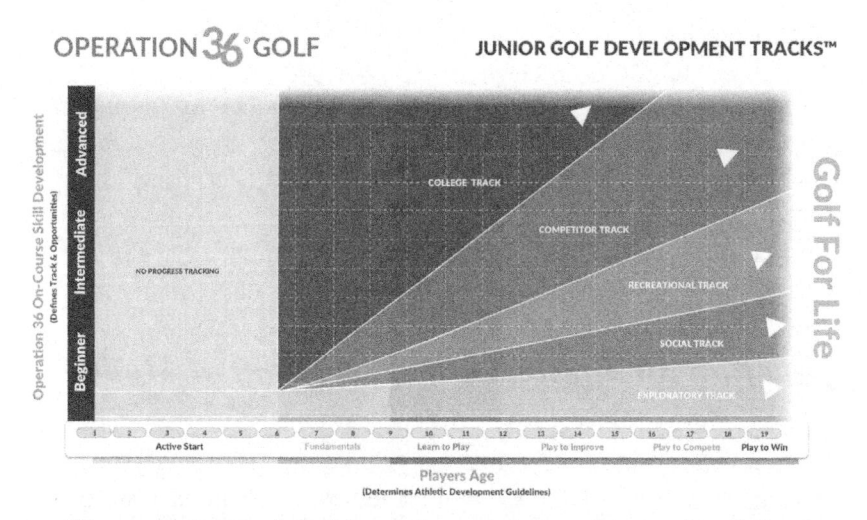

Figure 8: On the left side of the graph (y-axis) are the different stages of golfer development based on the Operation 36 on-course development model. As a player beats 36 at the different yardages, they move up the vertical axis. The three

stages are labeled in the diagram above as Beginner, Intermediate and Advanced.

The challenge is that progress in Junior Golf Development has always been a bit of a mystery. If a Junior wants to play golf in college, are they on track? The answers to those questions were always so vague, we as coaches admit to providing the muddiest of answers over the years. We never had a good answer until the creation of the Operation 36 Junior Golf Development Model.

The Goals

There are two goals of the Operation 36 Junior Golf Development Model: First, we want Juniors to play golf and sports for life, which is why we support the Long Term Athlete Development/American Development Model Guidelines (LTAD/ADM). (ADM, 2021)

These are research based guidelines from some of the smartest minds in Athlete Development in the world. These guide coaches and families to do the right thing at the right time for a Junior golfer. These principles were outlined earlier in the seven stages and key factors we use from LTAD/ADM. This is listed on the x-axis of the Operation 36 Junior Golf Development Model above.

Second, we want Juniors to be in positive golf environments that can give them the programming necessary to help them achieve their golf goals. This is the best way to help guide our Junior golfers as they develop their overall athletic and golf skills.

How it Works

Operation 36 golf coaches are equipped with the Junior Golf Development Reporting features in their Operation 36 Web

Platform. They have on-demand access to this report and can adjust the report in real time when meeting with families.

We highly recommend that when a Junior is ready to select a "Track Goal," they meet with their coach at least once per year to evaluate progress. The best time is usually at the start or end of each season. To repeat, the choice of this Track Goal is 100% the student's decision. Certainly, a parent or coach can help guide a player, but ultimately it is the student's decision.

When your Junior is ready, they can select a "Player" Track Goal, we refer to it as "My Motivation" on the player report. Why is the Junior playing golf? What interests the Junior? Every new golfer starts on the Golf Exploratory Track. After some time in the sport, and only if they wish to, they can adjust the track. The "My Motivation" Track can be changed at any time and is adjusted in real-time.

A player's Track Goal that they choose may not match up to the skill level they are demonstrating, and that is okay. We would say that is fairly normal.

For example, a player may choose the Social Track as they enjoy playing golf due to meeting new friends. However, they may be on pace to play on the College Track, based on the skill level they have demonstrated on the course. Again, the Junior Golf Development Model is in place to show a player what is possible, and this player may evolve into wanting to play in college at some point.

Based on their golf skill and age, coaches can see the actual Track. First, by understanding the player's age, we can recommend Athlete Development training guidelines (x-axis). Second, the Golf Skill Level of the player (My Skill Level) at their age will determine the actual golf development track they are on (y-axis).

Coaches can recommend specific programs and training plans. Based on your Juniors' goals, your coach can see if they are on track. If a player is ahead of pace or on pace it will motivate the Juniors to continue to do what they are doing, it is working. If they are behind pace, coaches can help guide programming plans to help catch up or possibly set more attainable goals.

Operation 36 Junior Golf Development Tracks

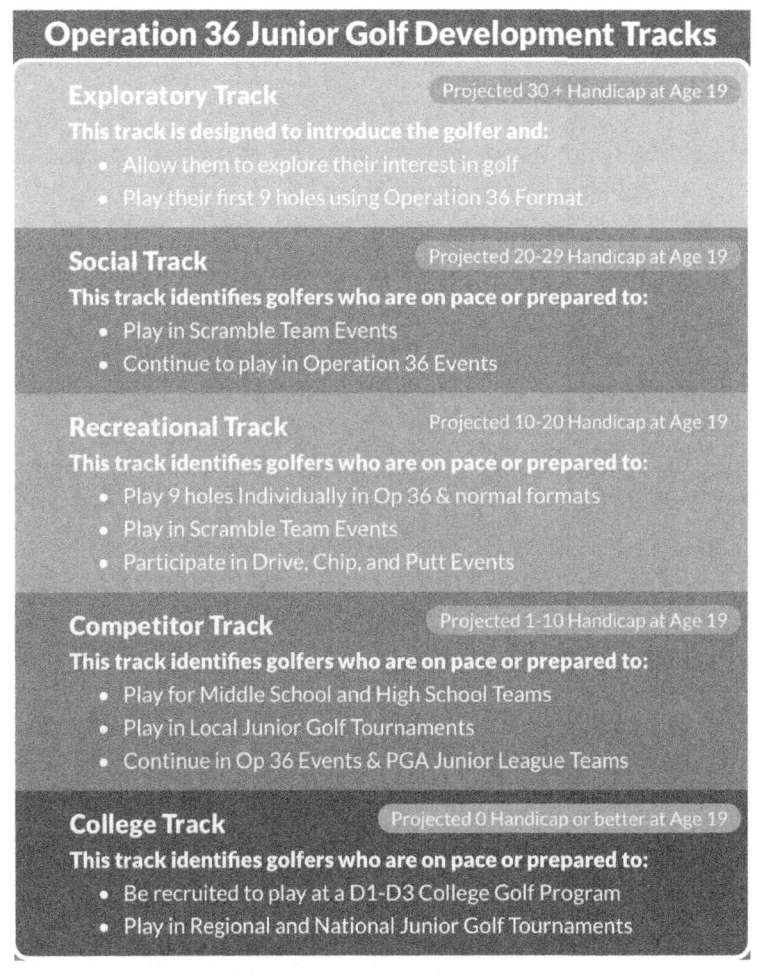

Exploratory Track
Projected 30+ Handicap at Age 19

This track is designed to introduce the golfer and:
- Allow them to explore their interest in golf
- Play their first 9 holes using Operation 36 Format

Social Track
Projected 20-29 Handicap at Age 19

This track identifies golfers who are on pace or prepared to:
- Play in Scramble Team Events
- Continue to play in Operation 36 Events

Recreational Track
Projected 10-20 Handicap at Age 19

This track identifies golfers who are on pace or prepared to:
- Play 9 holes Individually in Op 36 & normal formats
- Play in Scramble Team Events
- Participate in Drive, Chip, and Putt Events

Competitor Track
Projected 1-10 Handicap at Age 19

This track identifies golfers who are on pace or prepared to:
- Play for Middle School and High School Teams
- Play in Local Junior Golf Tournaments
- Continue in Op 36 Events & PGA Junior League Teams

College Track
Projected 0 Handicap or better at Age 19

This track identifies golfers who are on pace or prepared to:
- Be recruited to play at a D1-D3 College Golf Program
- Play in Regional and National Junior Golf Tournaments

Figure 9: The five player tracks in the Operation 36 Junior Golf Development Model.

Here is a brief description of each player track. For even more detail on this, please find your local Operation 36 coach who can help guide you in your Junior's current track.

Exploratory Track

This track defines players who are just testing the sport. It is important with these players that we are focused on making them feel competent quickly, getting them connected with a peer group, and giving them a vision for what might lie ahead in golf.

Playing group training games with no winners and losers and learning to feel empowered is important with this group. Having autonomy and choice to make their own decisions in golf is incredibly important to this group.

Social Track

This track defines players who are somewhat more connected to the sport. They enjoy coming to classes to see their friends as their primary driver. They enjoy playing games in classes and like group settings compared with doing private lessons or solo-based training activities. They enjoy learning and improving, but are not very motivated by goal setting and get more enjoyment out of being around others.

In these types of players, you may see they enjoy listening in classes and being with their friends, but might care less about wanting to show you their Level 1 Posture skill to earn a skill objective. This is okay, because they are still learning, but don't value accomplishing goals or milestones. Let them have fun with their friends, and little by little, the environment may steer them toward wanting to improve their own game, which brings us to the next track.

Recreational Track

This track defines players who are now starting to identify as golfers and are motivated to improve their personal game. They enjoy achievements and setting goals. They enjoy shooting low scores on the golf course or breaking personal bests. Earning a badge as a symbol for accomplishing goals is a great game mechanic to keep these golfers motivated.

These are the golfers who appreciate the narrative and have a vision for where they want to be. They like to work on their games in group activities, but also enjoy individual work on their game. As they develop skills, the more motivated they become. They tend to like competition with themselves, versus competition against others. Team games are still a good way to motivate this group, as a majority of golfers prefer social interaction when training and playing.

Competitive Track

This track defines players who love playing golf to compete. They love winning. They want to take their skills they have earned and try to beat their opponent. Typically, we don't reach this level until our skills are more developed. However, it is common to get a beginner who is on the competitive track.

These Juniors are motivated in other sports and activities by winning. It is important that you are setting realistic goals and placing these players in environments where they can experience success and have a chance to win. When they are training, they are not training to train for themselves, they are training to win! They are okay training in groups and enjoy working on their game individually as well.

Collegiate Track

The final track for Junior golfers is the collegiate track. This is for skilled players who want to play at the highest level of amateur golf. These players tend to be skilled and are driven to win. They enjoy playing against others and competing so much that they want to go to school and play on a team. They may have aspirations to play professionally as well.

These players, as we explained in previous chapters, need to have pure intrinsic intentions to be in this track. It is okay if we paint a vision of playing college golf using role models and stories, but if coaches or parents are the ones pushing this track early, the player will never be successful. A player who is in this track will be ready to ramp up training and is going to be more apt to want to be training more individually under the watchful eye of a coach. It is not easy to play at the top level, so that intrinsic motivation is a must. This comes from having complete autonomy and an environment where they know they have everything they need to improve and get to the next level.

Supporting Your Junior

As you are developing your golfer, it is important to know what track they are on so you can best support them. The Operation 36 Junior Development Track feature allows students to select their track goal so it keeps everyone on the same page. Based on their selected track, we now know what we can do to best support a player.

Just remember, as players develop, their interests and player track will fluctuate. Sometimes, we may be motivated to play competitively, and a few months later, we just want to play with friends. Our interests change over the course of time due to many factors.

When a Junior golfer has a clear path to their goal, they are more motivated to do what it takes to improve their game. The Junior Golfer Development Model is a tool to help coaches and parents to guide the training and practice for the Junior, based on their motivation for playing golf.

Becoming a Golfer: Stories from Operation 36 Coaches

Jonathan Rodriguez – Began Operation 36 at 10 years old
Coach: Marc Lapointe – Marc Lapointe Golf Academy, Fort Mill, South Carolina

Jonathan had tried all other organized sports before finding himself at an Operation 36 new student orientation in the spring of 2018. His parents, like many others, were simply hoping to find a sport their son would find interesting and stick with for more than a few weeks before wanting to quit.

After listening to what the program was about, meeting the staff, and with a bit of coaxing from his parents and his potential new golf coaches, he agreed to give golf a try.

A few weeks later, Jonathan arrived at his first class with a positive attitude, but quickly got discouraged with how different and difficult this new sport was. Armed with a structured curriculum and the Operation 36 Mobile App, the coaching staff helped to build his confidence and technique over that first semester and he was able to pass *three* Levels. His usual shy demeanor had turned into a quiet confidence. Jonathan was having fun! He really enjoyed learning about all aspects of the game.

Much to his parents' delight, he asked to be enrolled into that summer's Operation 36 program, and then the fall program and then again in the winter! By his one year anniversary of joining our Operation 36 classes, he had passed three playing levels and was halfway through Level 4.

Jonathan is now a member of his high school varsity golf team, has played TPC Sawgrass on a family trip, and loves researching golf history. He has helped his community raise money through school sponsored charity golf events and still practices regularly.

Currently, Jonathan is in Level 6 and volunteers his Saturday mornings giving back to the program by assisting the golf academy during supervised practices.

The Operation 36 Program has helped Jonathan and hundreds of others become skilled, lifelong golfers!

Becoming a Golfer: In their Coaches Words

Olivia Carter – began at 11 years old
Coach: Jill Finlan Scally, LPGA – Scally Golf Academy, Moon Township, Pennsylvania

Olivia began her journey with Operation 36 in 2018. She was one of our first students in the program. Olivia had been a student of ours previously and passed from Level 1 – 25 yards on her first attempt, and Level 2 – 50 yards on her second attempt. She passed from Level 3 on her third attempt.

Olivia hit her challenge point at Level 4. She has made 24 attempts to pass Level 4. Throughout this time, Olivia has grown so much as a golfer. She has had many ups and downs, but has persevered. Olivia's putting has improved from an average of 20 to 23 putts per nine holes to around 15 to 18 putts per nine. At other tournaments, she is often complimented on her great short game.

Olivia has never once talked about quitting. She even received a hand written letter of encouragement from Ryan Dailey commending her for her efforts. She knows that she is getting better all the time and learning from each match.

Olivia has won numerous tournaments in the last two years and shot in the 70s in a tournament for the first time this past summer. She is currently in seventh grade. Olivia has goals to try out for the high school golf team in ninth grade, and she would eventually like to play college golf. Operation 36 has contributed greatly to her development as a competitive golfer and improved her determination.

Chapter 9: The Role of Parents

Over the years, we have worked with numerous parents to support their Junior golfer. Supporting a child with sports can be a bit tricky. Although you did not receive a manual for how to raise your children, consider this your manual to help your Junior with their journey with golf!

As you learned, the scores your Junior shoots in the Operation 36 nine-hole events will look more like a roller coaster than a straight line! That is normal. This would be a similar roller coaster if you tracked a player's scores in all of their Junior tournaments, or even on the PGA Tour. Graphs of golf scores all look the same, we've just created software for the coach, parents and players to see it clearly.

We've taken the confusion out of what is about to happen in this journey with your child by compiling data over the years. On this roller coaster of improvement, all hands are needed to help a player. Being aware of the 'ups and downs' beforehand can help a parent and coach best prepare for how they can help.

Further, if you enrolled in the program as an adult, this is what your scores would look like once you reached a challenging yardage. That is what learning looks like!

T.R. - 10 years old
9-Hole Event Journey
150 YARDS

OPERATION 36° GOLF

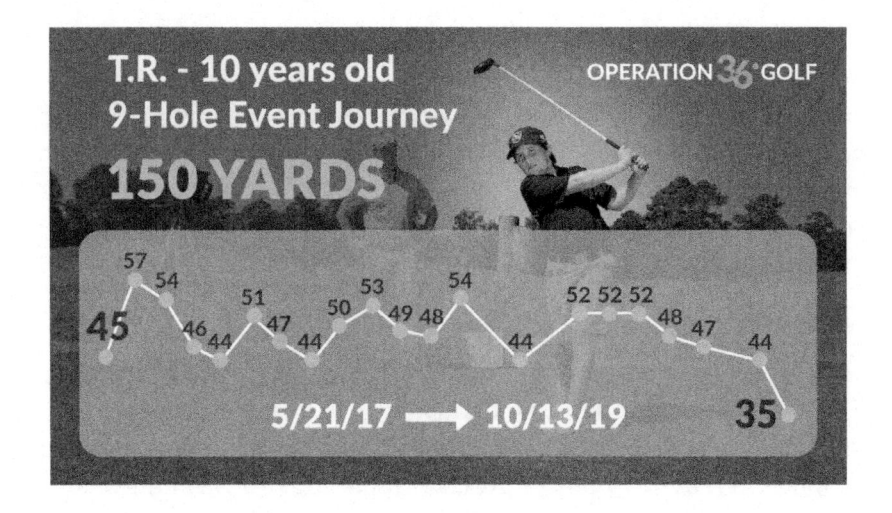

57, 54, 45, 46, 44, 51, 47, 44, 50, 53, 49, 48, 54, 44, 52, 52, 52, 48, 47, 44, 35

5/21/17 → 10/13/19

If a player takes 20 attempts to beat 36, which is very normal, the first 19 attempts are rich and full of learning experiences. Each time out they are learning new ways to approach shots, different clubs to use and areas of their game that they need to improve.

Yes, they would all include an unintended outcome of not beating 36, but the experts in learning encourage athletes to get out of their comfort zone and embrace the struggle. As you likely know, the struggle is where learning takes place. It is where character skills are built that will help them in golf, as well as other areas of life.

These unintended outcomes are required learning experiences. As a beginning golfer, no one has picked up a golf club and passed every yardage in their first attempt. It just doesn't happen.

As a parent, if you know that 95% of the time, your Junior will most likely not beat 36. How could they have fun in the 95%? How could you help them document what lessons they learn in each round as they build the skills to eventually beat 36?

Well, we highly recommend you don't expect them to beat 36 in a less than "normal" rate and accidentally use body language, tone and words to make them feel like they have let you down.

As you know, children grow and develop at different rates. We recommend that if your Junior hits a bad shot, round or is in a slump, be slow to react. Know that these "hiccups" are all normal and part of the journey. This is not a sprint for short term on-course wins, it is a marathon to develop both on-course skills and life skills over time.

70% of Kids Quit Sports By the Age of 13

The fact that 70% of kids quit sports by the age of 13 is a great signal to us to evaluate the role of adults in youth sports. Maybe we should consider adjusting *what we are currently doing* to lower this percentage and help more youth continue to enjoy all the benefits of participating in sports?

Certainly, kids age out and move on to other things, however it might be helpful for us to reflect on what we are currently doing to help those that are leaving at such a young age.

What do kids learn in sports?

As we decide whether to invest time, effort and energy into guiding our kids to stay in sports, what is the benefit? Author and parent Julianna W. Miner, in a 2016 Washington Post article, said, "Playing sports offers everything from physical activity, experiencing success and bouncing back from failure to taking calculated risks and dealing with the consequences to working as a team and getting away from the ubiquitous presence of screens." (Miner, 2016)

Her conclusion was that sports are an amazing arena to develop foundational life skills. The truth is that 70% of kids quit sports by the age of 13 and the top reason given why they quit is, "It wasn't fun anymore."

In that same 2016 Washington Post article, Miner offers up this solution: "So why do 70 percent of kids quit organized sports at 13 and what can we do about it? I would argue that most kids leave because we (adults) haven't given them a way to stay. And perhaps more importantly, until we dismantle the parenting culture that emphasizes achievement and success over healthy, happy kids, we don't stand a chance of solving this problem."

At Operation 36, we are focused on helping improve that percentage and keep more kids in sports, specifically in golf. In fact, our goal is for them to fall in love with golf at a young age and continue playing for the rest of their lives.

As parents, there are three specific ways that you can support an encouraging, fun environment for your children. The first is to remove expectations from your Junior and golf. If they are in an Operation 36 program, they will have the best possible curriculum available, and one that focuses on their overall development. Understand that your reaction to each shot has a tremendous impact on your Junior's overall experience. You don't need to worry about coaching your golfer, the coach will be able to fill that role. When parents are supportive and encouraging, rather than having high expectations on the course, the Junior will have a much better experience.

Next, we would recommend that saying less is more, especially if you are caddying for your Junior. Your child does not want to disappoint you, and you may say something that could impact your child's view of their performance.

Finally, share with your Junior how much you enjoy watching them play. This one phrase can replace the tension and expectations that come along with sports and can replace it with fun.

The Truth about Sports Parents...

One of the most popular videos that we share with our parents when they first join an Operation 36 program that we run here in North Carolina and Virginia is the video titled, "The Truth about Sports Parents..." on YouTube. It's a great way to help shape our mindsets as parents as to what our kids would prefer we do to support them in sporting events versus what we end up doing without even thinking about. (*The Truth About Sports Parents...*, 2016)

Whether we like it or not, we as parents are a major influence on whether our child has a positive experience or a negative experience in golf. What we say and do can either drive them away from the sport or motivate them to stay.

Your Words Matter

Here are some of the most powerful responses in the video. The kids in the video range in age from 5 to 15 years old. They play sports ranging from baseball to volleyball to basketball and many others.

The producers asked kids to say how they feel when their parents watch their sporting events. They replied:

- "I prefer my parents if I play bad, don't say anything, and if I play well, it doesn't really matter if they compliment me on how I play. I just, like, I don't know I prefer my parents not talk as much."

- "(In the game) I can hear them (parents) cheering me on and I'm like thinking in my head "just shut it I'm trying to focus."

- "She tells me to get in the position that my coach told me not to get in. I'm like, 'Well, No' and then she's like, 'Get in your position' and I'm like, 'No.'"

- "Coming from the coach's mouth is kind of better I feel like, because your parents are there to support you and your coach is there to help you, you know."

- "They don't need to like always be like telling me what to do like every minute of the game they kind of just gotta let me play."

When asked what they prefer from their parents:

- "I'd like to look back and I'd like to see you like, smile, or like, give me a thumbs up."

- "Mom, I wish you would be a little bit quieter."

- "Say, like, 'You play(ed) good and you can get them next time.'"

- "I want you to know I need big hugs."

- "I love the nights when you bring me (to practice)."

- "What makes me happy (is) when you always encourage me."

- "Please, just be my Mom and Dad."

Hopefully you can see how well-meaning words from parents can be received as pressure by their children. They end the video by sharing that the only thing they need to hear you say is, "I love to watch you play."

Fun Changes With Age

Fun can change for a player as they age. What was fun for a child in golf at age 8 usually evolves into something different at age 12 and age 16. Be aware of this and adapt your level of support to support their definition of fun.

8 Years Old

At age 8, it might be fun for your child to practice the Operation 36 curriculum skills at your house and mark off the objectives as they complete them. This might involve you reviewing the curriculum video in the Operation 36 app and helping your child practice the skill. It might involve you reaching out to the coach for clarification on a particular skill your child is having trouble mastering.

Fun for an 8 year old usually also involves coming home and wanting to play the same games they did in class with you. This might involve you picking up a club in the backyard, basement or play area and participating with them. For some families, this can lead to a daily time when you get to spend time with your junior and learn all the games they are playing in class. We've been through this stage with our kids, and it is a really fun stage to be a parent and participate in.

12 Years Old

At age 12, your child might be motivated by improving their on-course skills trying to beat 36. This might involve you taking your child to the course to train either at the practice facility or on the course on a regular basis. It might mean choosing one or two specific days a week that you devote to playing with your child after you get home from work.

When this happens, a common thing we see is parents practicing from the same on-course yardage as their child. A child might be playing from Level 3 – 100 yards and the parent drops a ball next to them and plays the same yardage for nine holes. Fun has evolved from learning skills and playing games at age 8 to possibly wanting to improve their skills on the course at age 12.

At this age, children will also enjoy attending a PGA or LPGA Tour event where they can get up close and see the professionals. We highly recommend trying to go to one of these events on a Thursday morning, as the crowds are usually smaller and the players are very approachable. Ryan attended a recent Symetra Tour event (the LPGA's "minor league" tour) with his daughter, and countless players approached her and started a conversation. She received over a half-dozen golf balls from players that signed them. On the way home, she asked, "Dad, can we go to the course and practice tomorrow?" What a great experience!

16 Years Old

At age 16, your Junior may be playing in high school and Junior tournaments. They may have progressed to a level where they can beat you on a regular basis. This would be a time for you to buckle down, take some lessons and train some more so you can compete with your Junior. Fun for the two of you may be taking a weekend golf trip together, playing in the weekly morning game at your golf course with the regulars, and entering into Adult/Junior events together.

When your Junior is playing in tournaments, your role may turn into statistician as you keep stats for them while they are playing. At dinner after the round, you may turn into a part time sports psychologist as you try to help your Junior move on from a tough shot or round and look forward to the next opportunity.

When in Doubt

We suspect that if you are invested enough in reading a book to support your Junior Golfer, you are committed to their success and overall happiness. Your Junior is very lucky to have you on their support team!

As long as you are putting them in a positive environment, with an engaging curriculum with a vision for success, you are on the right track. Rest assured knowing that the coaching can be done by the Golf Coach, and your main role is to support. You can achieve this with a smile, encouragement, "thumbs up" or the classic line, "I love to watch you play."

Becoming a Golfer: Stories from Operation 36 Coaches

Michael Snyder – Began Operation 36 at 5 years old
Coach: Ryan Dailey – Keith Hills Golf Academy, Buies Creek, NC

The secret to success in golf is perseverance and Michael's journey is a shining example of this. As a junior golfer, Michael was always a little smaller than most, didn't win any of our physical contests we had in class and didn't hit the ball very far. His secret was he never gave up and to this day he keeps on showing up and putting in the work.

Michael started with us at the young age of 5 and graduated from Operation 36 by beating Level 10 when he was 14 years old. He attended weekly classes, 9-hole events and private lessons for almost 10 years. His journey has given us a great understanding of what it takes to get through all 10 levels of the Operation 36 program and the support that is needed from coaches, players and parents along the way.

Operation 36 has provided him the perfect environment to get his reps in playing on the course in a tournament-like atmosphere. In total, Michael played in 149 Operation 36 9-hole events over his 10 years in the program.

At times in Operation 36, a player will reach a yardage that is very challenging for them. This is normal and it will take them multiple attempts to build the skills to beat 36. Michael's journey is no different.

At Level 5 - 200 yards, his first score was a 49 which meant he needed to improve by at least 13 strokes. At the time, Michael hit his driver maybe 100-110 yards so for the first time he was challenged to hit the fairway and then have an accurate approach shot. It took him 22 attempts at Level 5 to beat 200 yards over an 18 month period of time.

At Level 7 2301-2600 yards, his first score was a 46. Again he needed to improve by double digits, 10 strokes. For most facilities, Level 7 is the senior tees or 2nd set of tees. It took Michael 64 attempts and over 2 years to build the skills necessary to beat 36 from Level 7.

Did he have times he wanted to give up? Absolutely.

Did he give up? No, he kept playing, putting in the reps and trying to get better with the coaching staff round after round, month after month and year after year.

We have always wanted Operation 36 to be the local option for families to get their junior started in the game without having to travel the state for tournaments and shell out a lot of money for tournament fees. Michael's journey is a great example of a family staying at their home course and using Operation 36 as the vehicle to get in the reps needed to improve over a 10 year period of time.

This summer, he turned 15 years old and came within 1 shot of qualifying for the US Junior Amateur in Bandon Dunes. This summer he shot tournament rounds of 67-66-68 and his lowest score ever on his home course of 65. He has risen from ranked 130th in the state at the beginning of the summer to currently 37th and he is nationally ranked in the top 800 players in the country.

In total, Michael played in 149 Operation 36 9-hole events and lost 57 strokes in his 10 years in the program. Because he has been playing a golf course that is scaled to his skill, he has always shot rounds around par and has gotten used to going low. He is a great example of how shooting low scores as a junior on a course that is the appropriate yardage for your skill can significantly help a player as they graduate into junior tournaments and move on to play in college.

Michael gives back to the Academy by volunteering to coach and mentor many of the players that are following in his footsteps. When a player comes back from a 9-hole event and is feeling down after a tough round, Michael jumps in to share his story to help inspire and motivate them to keep working hard and not give up. Everything you ever want is on the other side of hard.

Chapter 10: Next Steps

Hopefully by this point, you are able to see the science and heart behind the Operation 36 program, and you feel well equipped to support your Junior in their golf journey.

Giving your Junior the gift of learning how to play golf on the course and providing them an environment that will motivate them to want to improve is, in our opinion, priceless!

Learning to play golf can open up so many opportunities for Juniors. Of course there are future applications, but most immediately, we love seeing Juniors learn how to set goals. And achieve them! We love seeing their own view of themselves change because of their persistence and determination. Finally, we love seeing their confidence improve both on and off the course. All of this is possible if they have the right program and the right support.

"When we teach people how their learning machine (brain) actually works – and that creativity, innovation, and growth ALL come from the obstacles, challenges, set backs, and changes that lead to desirable struggle... We can start to seek out those situations – and struggle on purpose... Which is exactly what great learners (Jungle Tigers) do." - Trevor Ragan

When we began creating a program that was built around how people actually love to learn, and one that embraced the appropriate challenges, it was like wildfire that could not be stopped!

Our vision for the future of golf is that every new golfer will start in a local Operation 36 program. They will **play** in nine-hole events on a regular basis, **train** in weekly small group classes with a curriculum and be motivated along the way with the support of technology to guide both the coach and player.

Now you have the education, resources and understanding of how to create a Junior golfer! We are hopeful that golf will be a rewarding part of your Junior's life, and that it will be a sport your entire family can enjoy.

If your family is not currently in an Operation 36 program, we would love to invite you to find a local program.

How Do I Get Involved In a Program or Use Operation 36?

As of the writing of this book, the best way to get involved is to find a local program near you. Go to www.operation36.golf, click on 'Find a Program' and reach out to your local coach.

You can learn more about the programs they offer, the time of year they are offered, and many other details on our website. Please be aware that some programs are offered at private golf clubs that require you to be a member. Usually another program is available within the area that is open to the public.

Thank You!

What started as a two-person operation that was on the brink of failure has blossomed into a global program with nearly 100,000 golfers, with a clear mission to create 1 million golfers.

Our hardworking team has expanded over the past few years, and we are so thankful to the coaches and families who were open to learning golf a new way…backwards!

Yes–after some time, we are, in fact, very thankful for the 40 families who quit our early golf coaching. We may never have discovered there was a much more effective way to become a golfer! We are so happy to have your family as a part of the Operation 36 community. Together, we are changing the way golf is taught and played.

Appendix A: Parent's Checklist

Complete Program Checklist

Use this checklist as you research programs online and in-person to figure out which golf program is the best for your family or for someone you are guiding into the sport. We believe that these items are the most important for delivering a complete program for beginner golfers.

Operation 36 Golf Program

- Developmental Program with a Plan
- Participants Play Golf
- On-Course Development Model
- Golfer Curriculum / Educational Plan
- Progress Tracking
- Tech Guided Training
- Relationships & Community

Traditional Golf Program

- Drop-In Clinic or Seasonal Camp with no Plan
- No Golf Included
- No Model to Learn to Play
- No Long-Term Plan Used
- No Progress Tracking
- No Tech for Coach or Student
- Short-Term Relationships

Appendix B: What Will My Junior Learn At Each Level?

This answer could fill an entire book on its own. We will try to give you a condensed answer here and then if you want even more, please reach out to your local Operation 36 coach.

As you participate in the Operation 36 program, you will learn different skills in each yardage level. The beauty of it is that the skills you learn at each level will build on each other to help you at each future level. Here is a "reader's digest" version of what skills you can commonly expect to learn at each level:

Level 1 – 25 yards

1 – Rules and Etiquette Skills

The bulk of the learning in Level 1 – 25 yards is in learning how the game is played for a beginner golfer. Similar to every other sport, the sport of golf has rules and general practices which are referred to as golf etiquette. These are designed to make the game of golf safer and more enjoyable to all while decreasing the chance for damage to the course, golf equipment and others. Mastering these fundamental skills in rules and etiquette will prepare someone to be able to play golf with anyone for the rest of their lives.

We would share that the biggest challenge in helping a beginner golfer is that 99% of the time, a coach is trying to teach these rules and etiquette skills **without ever getting on the course** with the player. They hand out a flier and read it in a classroom with a player, or do an exercise on the training facility grounds demonstrating it or on a whiteboard.

According to the learning pyramid below, **this would be considered "passive learning," and the retention rate can range from 30% to as low as 5%.** In most cases, coaches never cover this area with a student and leave it up to them to learn on their own.

As far as learning is concerned, nothing replaces actually playing the game and learning on the course. Why? It helps both the new player and the experienced player. When the beginner golfer is on the course, practicing skills by performing them on the playing field, the retention rate soars as high as 75% – much better than the under 30% when a flier is handed out or a demonstration is observed.

The Learning Pyramid

Average Retention Rates

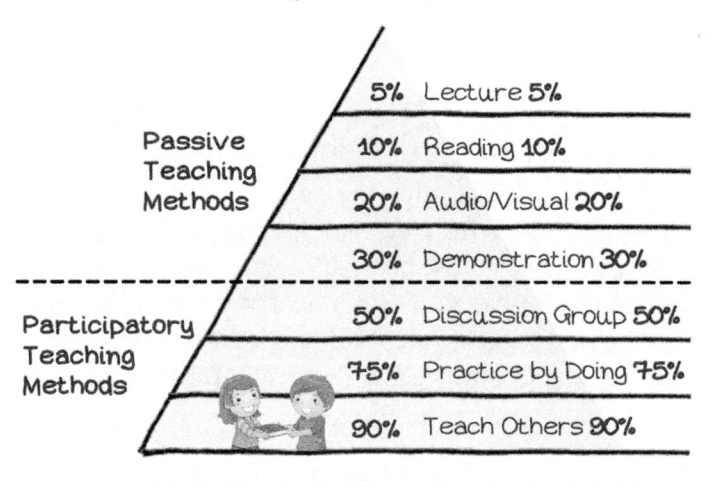

Passive Teaching Methods
- 5% Lecture 5%
- 10% Reading 10%
- 20% Audio/Visual 20%
- 30% Demonstration 30%

Participatory Teaching Methods
- 50% Discussion Group 50%
- 75% Practice by Doing 75%
- 90% Teach Others 90%

Adapted from National Training Laboratories. Bethel, Maine

Want the greatest return? Fast forward to after a few nine-hole events, when someone knows a thing or two about playing. When the experienced player teaches the new player on the course or in class, the experienced player learns at the highest rate (90%). *Teaching others requires the highest level of understanding.* As Operation 36 coaches, we look for opportunities to facilitate a player teaching another player what they have learned previously or from experience.

2 – Golf Skills

From 25 yards away, one main golf skill will be learned.

Touch

Touch is the ability to control how far the ball goes. Many of us may initially think that the most important skill in golf is to hit the ball as far as possible. Yes, that is needed, and will be learned. However, the skill of stopping the ball is actually the most important skill to learn early on in a player's development. How hard do I need to hit this for it to stay on the green or stop close to the hole? And at each successive level in Operation 36, a player's touch will need to improve for them to build the skills to beat 36.

That's the "secret sauce" behind why Operation 36 works so well. Touch is a requirement at each level yardage and it needs to improve each time you move back. When someone graduates from Operation 36 by beating all 10 level yardages, they have developed over time a level of touch in the game that will help them for the rest of their lives. Think about learning how to shoot a basketball. The skills you learned as a beginner, still help you to this day. Very few players that played basketball on a consistent basis as a youngster have trouble hitting the rim later in life. Whereas if you meet someone who has never played basketball struggles to hit the rim on a consistent basis.

No matter how hard you work on your swing and hitting the ball far, when you arrive in and around the green you will need to have touch to stop the ball close to the hole. As an example, the best players in the world – those that practice everyday, get paid millions of dollars playing golf, have the best equipment, best coaches and play on the nicest courses – leave the ball on average 37 feet, 3 inches from the hole on every hole after they've hit the ball towards the green. Yes, almost 40 feet away!

They leave the ball nearly 40 feet away from the hole, and they are the best players in the world. They understand this and dedicate hours and hours to practicing their short game shots within 25 yards of the green.

To a seasoned golfer or coach, when they see someone in Operation 36, they are amazed at how good their touch is around the greens. They are blown away that someone who is new to the game has learned how to stop the ball relatively close to the hole when they are within 25 yards of the green.

Why are they blown away? It's not normal. Most golfers have little to no touch.

The large majority of golfers, those who may have played their entire lives, struggle with touch. They either never put in the time to develop it (No. 1 reason) or they used to have good touch and have not focused their practice time on it. Why didn't they put in the time to develop it?

It wasn't a priority. They started playing from the tee box and they focused the majority of their time on figuring out how to advance the ball off the tee. The last thing they did on a hole was hit shots around the green so that was the last thing they had time to work on.

These are the same players that hit the ball reasonably well off the tee and then struggle around the greens.

Think back to our discussion in Chapter 1 about repetitions and how important that is to a player's development. By starting out in Level 1 – 25 yards, a player will play nine holes with their primary focus on figuring out how hard they need to hit the ball to stop it close to the hole – touch. And if it takes them more than 36 strokes, which it does for 99.9% of beginners, they are then challenged to repeat playing from 25 yards until they can develop the skills to shoot 36 or better.

Golf skills learned in Level 1 – 25 yards include:
- Touch
- Club Selection: What club should I use? What club should I not use?
- Short and Long Putting
- Chipping from the fairway
- Marking the ball
- Where to walk on the putting green
- Pace of Play
- What to wear
- What to say
- What not to say

Level 2 – 50 yards

1 – Rules/Etiquette

The majority of the rules/etiquette were experienced from Level 1 – 25 yards. At each successive yardage a player will continue to refine their understanding and demonstration of these skills. It's fantastic for players to learn the foundation in Level 1 and be able to practice it at each successive level. By the time a player graduates from Operation 36, they will be as good as anyone on the course (probably better than most) with their understanding and demonstration of rules/etiquette.

2 – Golf Skills

Juniors – From 50 yards away, the younger players will be starting to make a full swing with something similar to a 7-iron or maybe even a wood. For the older players, they will be making a less than full swing with a wedge.

Adults – From 50 yards away, most adults will be making a less than full swing with a wedge.

As larger swings are used, larger errors will occur. Areas around the green that were not in play at 25 yards will certainly be in play from 50 yards and beyond. One such area is the bunker or sand trap. Bunkers are the sand-filled areas next to a green. For beginner players, it is very helpful for them to learn how to get out of bunkers early on in their development. Many seasoned veterans in the game fear hitting in bunkers as they have never learned how to get out of them.

In addition to the touch around the greens that will continue to be mastered, a player will start to learn how to execute a shot of around 50 yards. They will learn in the Operation 36 curriculum that one of the most important fundamentals is hitting the ball first. Many times, beginners think that hitting the ground before the ball is how the golf club is used. Unfortunately, the golf club is built to strike the ball first and then possibly the ground after depending on the particular shot played.

Players will also start to learn basic clubface control. The ball generally starts in the direction that the clubface is pointed at impact. Players learn this and practice this in Level 1 of the Operation 36 curriculum. They hit shots purposely to the right, left and then straight to experience the different feels. They do this on a consistent basis in class so that they can improve to a point where they can make adjustments when they are on the course.

Getting comfortable with a 50-yard shot is certainly helpful from Level 2 and it is also very helpful when a player reaches the tee box. No matter how good a player they are, they will hit the ball in trouble or in the trees from the tee box at some point. When a player is in the trees, they usually have two choices. If they have an opening, they can hit it up to the green. If they don't, they can hit back out into the fairway and leave a shot of usually around 50 to 100 yards on a par 4.

We have seen players that are not comfortable hitting a 50-yard shot try to aggressively play through a small opening to get the ball up to the green. Many times, it ends up hitting a branch, dropping straight down or deflecting out of bounds. By getting comfortable hitting 50-yard shots early on in a player's development, it will certainly give them more options as they move back in yardage.

Golf skills learned in Level 2 – 50 yards include:
- "Tee" shots:
    - Touch
    - Contact
    - Direction
    - Club Selection: What club should I use? What club should I not use?
- Approach shots
    - All shots from within 25 yards are used
        - Chipping/Pitching from the fairway, rough and bunker
        - Short and Long Putts

Level 3 – 100 yards

1 – Rules/Etiquette

Players continue to practice the rules and etiquette when playing from Level 3 – 100 yards. Since they have played in multiple nine-hole events by this stage, the local coach may pair this player up with a beginner. This gives them an opportunity to teach someone else and help them.

This is another key moment in Operation 36 when a player gains in their confidence. When a coach asks an experienced player to guide a beginner in their first nine-hole event, you immediately see the experienced player's body language perk up. They gain a sense of excitement and accomplishment as they get to share what they learned with someone else. This is certainly a key moment we enjoy seeing all the time.

2 – Golf Skills

Power

At Level 3 – 100 yards most everyone is making a full swing at this point. Learning how to hit the ball far enough is certainly a focus at this stage. Without getting too technical, it is at this stage that a Coach starts to introduce different power sources to the golf swing. If a player has trouble hitting the ball 100 yards, it is usually due to the technique they are using. Fortunately, if a player is using the Operation 36 curriculum, they have learned most of the common power sources by this point and won't need to learn anything drastically new.

Strategy – The golf term is "course management"

What should my plan be? Where should I try to land this ball?

It could be argued that strategy is important at every yardage. However, it really starts to come into play at Level 3 and above. It is very helpful for us to understand that during the course of a 9-hole round of golf, even the best players only hit three or four shots that are struck perfectly and turn out exactly how they planned. What? Yes, for us in Operation 36 the average is closer to one or two shots that are hit perfectly and turn out exactly how we want it.

Golfing legend Ben Hogan said, "A good round (18 holes) of golf is when you can hit three shots that turn out exactly like you envision them before you swing the club."

If that is the case, attention needs to be focused on coming up with a strategy that allows a player to shoot the lowest score with the understanding that most shots won't go exactly as planned. A player will work with a coach to help them come up with this strategy.

At a very simple level, trying to hit your shots to the center of the green is a much more effective strategy than trying to hit the shot directly at the flagstick. When someone intentionally tries to hit a shot that is not in the center of the green, a large percentage of their missed shots will end up missing the green. However, when you try to hit the center of the green and ignore the hole, a large majority of your misses will still end up on the green.

For more information on this strategy of trying to hit your shots to the center of the green, please see your local Operation 36 coach. They would be more than happy to show you why this strategy for beginner golfers is the most effective. They also have access to the Operation 36 curriculum which goes into further detail on this very subject.

Golf skills learned in Level 3 – 100 yards include:
- Tee Shots:
    - Distance
    - Contact
    - Direction
    - Club Selection: What club should I use? What club should I not use?
- Approach shots:
    - All shots from within 25 yards are used
        - Chipping/Pitching from the fairway, rough and bunker
        - Short and Long Putts

Level 4 – 150 yards

1 – Rules/Etiquette

Players continue to practice the rules and etiquette when playing from Level 4 – 150 yards. In a typical Operation 36 program a player who is at Level 4 – 150 yards is certainly a role model that the younger or less experienced players look up to.

2 – Golf Skills

At Level 4, some players are hitting woods and even drivers. Stronger players might be hitting an iron or even a wedge from this distance. Remember back to our conversation about the 6:15 system of stat tracking? The 6 is the benchmark we are trying to meet or exceed for greens in regulation. Our definition of a green in regulation in Operation 36 is stopping our ball on the green in two shots or less.

With that in mind, this is a great yardage for players to start to understand the value of accuracy over power in your approach shots. For example, a player might be able to swing as hard as they can with a pitching wedge and get it to the green. However, they could take a slightly smaller and smoother swing with a 9-iron or 8-iron and be much more accurate more often. This conversation happens *all the time* at almost *every* Operation 36 program.

Why?

We are all wired to some degree to want to hit the ball as far as we possibly can. We want to be able to say we hit a pitching wedge 100 yards or 125 yards or 150 yards. For tee shots, we agree that distance is extremely important and helpful. The farther down the fairway you can hit the ball, the shorter the distance you have into the green. All things being equal, having a shorter shot into the green will leave you with a shorter putt to the hole on average.

How can a player find the best way to stop their ball on the green in two shots or less from 150 yards? This is an incredibly fun yardage to observe as a coach, parent or caddie. Players start to plan out shot No. 1 so that shot No. 2 is easier. That skill of planning out shot No. 1 to help shot No. 2 is never learned on the driving range or practice green. It can only be learned on the course with multiple reps of playing, learning and adjusting.

Maybe laying up to the front of the green and then chipping on is the best play?

Golf skills learned in Level 4 – 150 yards include:
- Tee Shots:
    - Touch
    - Contact
    - Direction
    - Club Selection – What club should I use? What club should I not use?
- Approach shots:
    - Short game shots out of the fairway, rough and other areas around the green
    - Bunker shots
    - Short and Long Putting

Level 5 – 200 yards

Rules/Etiquette

Players continue to practice the rules and etiquette when playing from Level 5 – 200 yards. More often than not, a coach will use a player at Level 5 to help explain rules/etiquette in class. It is also common for a coach to ask a player who is in Level 5 to caddie for a younger player.

Golf Skills

At Level 5 – 200 yards, most players in Operation 36 are hitting long irons and woods for their tee shot club if their goal is to get it on the green in one shot.

Something to think about:

"Approach shots account for the biggest scoring advantage between golfers of every skill level. The best golfers also gain strokes with their driving, short game and putting games, but approach shots are the greatest difference-maker." - Mark Broadie, author of *Every Shot Counts*

In Operation 36, your approach shot is your second shot. How can you then maximize your chances of stopping the ball on the green in two shots or less? We will share with you that 100% of players go for the green on all nine holes the first time they play from 200 yards. They figure out what club can get them on the green and then the strategy is to hit it on the green in one shot.

What happens? Big numbers.

Why? Some holes just don't have enough room up by the green to account for the dispersion that you will most likely have with a long iron or wood – and it is on these holes that players make the highest numbers.

For example, if a hole has water to the right of the green and out of bounds to the left of the green, statistically speaking you will hit it in the water or out of bounds a large percentage of the time. Whereas if you took the strategy on those holes to take less club off the tee and lay up to 25 yards in the fairway, you most likely will get your next shot on the green and two putt for par and may occasionally make birdie. This strategy certainly eliminates a 6, 7 or worse score.

Level 5 – 200 yards is a great yardage for a player to work with their coach to come up with the best strategy to give them the best chance each time they play. And the great thing about having regular nine-hole events is a player can experiment on certain strategies and learn what works best.

Golf skills learned in Level 5 – 200 yards include:

- Tee Shots:
    - Touch
    - Contact
    - Direction
    - Club selection: What club should I use? What club should I not use?
- Approach shots:
    - Short game shots out of the fairway, rough and other areas around the green
    - Bunker shots
    - Short and Long Putting

Levels 6-10 – 1801 yards to 3200+ yards

1 – Rules/Etiquette

Now that a player has worked their way back to the tee box, they simply use the rules/etiquette they have been practicing and learning in Levels 1 through 5.

2 – Golf Skills

Now that a player is at the tee box, they face longer and longer holes. This also brings in a very fun part of golf, different strategy on every hole which most players really enjoy.

In Operation 36, we honor each facility's definition of a par 3, 4 and 5 that is on the scorecard. Whereas in the previous yardages, Level 1 through 5, every hole is a par 4.

All of the golf skills learned up to this point are used to assist a player at the tee box. Most players have the physical skills at this point to be successful and will need to problem solve additional ways to improve.

Many times this includes improving a players ability to manage their emotions. If a player has truly gone through Levels 1 to 5 in a formal nine-hole event, they have had to already develop the ability to manage their emotions. Most likely, they faced some very challenging yardages along the way and had to persevere through.

Issues arise at this point if a player is just thrown into this position at the tee box without being given a chance to develop their skills previously. We highly recommend you follow whatever protocol your coach provides at your facility and not try to "fast forward" through any learning opportunities by skipping Level 1 to 5.

Unfortunately, we have heard a handful of stories over the years of players getting so frustrated when they get to the tee box in Operation 36 that they give up. As we dig further to learn why, we start to understand that these players did not go through the protocol of playing in nine-hole events starting at Level 1 and progressing. Somewhere along the way or even at the beginning, they were prevented from having those early learning opportunities by a coach or parent that "felt" they should be further along than they are.

Please, please, *please* adhere to the protocols that your coach prescribes as they are in the best interest of you or your Junior golfer. Fast forwarding them through a yardage is not helpful for the long term development of any player.

Final note: The Operation 36 model format of using a smaller than standard version of the sport is new to golf, but it's not new to other sports.

The strategy of training on a playing field that is smaller than the standard version to gain confidence and reps is what the most popular sports in the world already do. It works!

- Ice hockey uses a concept called 'cross-ice' where they shorten a normal 200-foot long ice rink into thirds, or 85-foot long surfaces. More players can fit on the ice at a

time because three separate games are going on at the same time, which allows them to get more reps shooting, passing and making decisions. With more reps, their confidence builds and their skills improve.
- Soccer (or football for most of you) has used futsal to help shrink the size of the field and increase the number of touches. With more touches, they have learned that confidence builds and skills improve. The great Brazilian players Zico, Pele and Socrates logged many hours playing futsal.
- Baseball has different field sizes for different ages. For example, a Little League field has base paths that measure 60 feet in length and a distance of 50 feet from the pitcher to the batter. This is designed for players ages 8 to 12. If you put this age group on a full-size field with base paths of 90 feet and 60 feet, 6 inches from the pitcher to the batter, everyone would be frustrated. A typical 8 year old can't even throw a ball 60 feet, 6 inches, and asking them to run 90 feet between bases is not a recipe for success.
- The NBA and USA Basketball released standard guidelines in 2018 for court size and height of the hoop along with several other age-appropriate recommendations to help players experience success and build their confidence. For example, a 7 or 8 year old plays on a court that is 50 feet by 42 feet with an 8-foot high hoop, whereas a 12 to 14 year old plays on a 94 foot by 50 foot court and uses a 10-foot high hoop.

Beginner golf programs have been stuck for many years. Very few have been willing to disrupt what has always been. Now there have been some outliers creating short courses and promoting players to start closer to the hole. However, no one has put in a system that could be easily used at every golf course around the world with no infrastructure costs to the course up until now.

Appendix C: Purpose – Micro vs. Macro

Every class with an Operation 36 golf coach has a purpose. Unfortunately, the majority of classes in the golf industry don't. Yes, it's sad but true. You might luck out and the coach in your program has a micro purpose for that class of getting better with your skill of putting or chipping. Or you might not, and you are just doing random things that the Coach saw another coach do on the internet and it fills the void of the 45-minute class.

Does the Program Have a Macro Purpose of Improving Your Game on the Golf Course?

Without a playing component with a Development model (macro purpose) in your program, players are left wandering in and out of clinics, private lessons and scouring the internet for help without having a clear understanding of how this will directly help them. Why am I doing this golf thing? Oh, to get better at golf. But I don't actually play golf on a regular basis, so why am I doing this?

Another good example of the power of progress is losing weight. The first pound to lose is the hardest as you start to change some of your habits. However, once you see that first pound lost on the scale you get a boost of motivation to keep doing what you're doing because it is working. You think, "Wow, in addition to drinking water instead of soda, I'm going to start working out." You start a snowball effect of making better and better choices and you start to lose more and more weight. It's the net effect of that first choice to drink water that compounds to 10 more better choices that lead to you reaching your goals.

Another example is a skateboard rider or scooter rider learning a new trick. If you've ever observed your child or someone else learning a new trick you know exactly what we are talking about. They are so excited when they get one step closer to landing a trick.

You can see it on their faces as the excitement builds. They'll run into the house with excitement when they've figured something out. "Dad, if I put my right hand here, it helps speed up the spin of the scooter and gets me closer to getting it around in time to land it."

It may take them two weeks, two months, or two years to land the trick. However, it was the little burst of excitement when they got closer and closer to landing it that motivated them to keep trying day after day.

Appendix D: Are There Recommended Carry Distance Benchmarks I Should Be Looking to Develop That Will Help Me Accomplish a Level?

Yes. Based on the PGA of America's Tee it Forward program, they have set forth guidelines on how far you should carry your driver to play a certain tee box. Here are the recommendations adapted for the 10 yardage levels for Operation 36:

1. Levels 1 to 3 – No recommendation
2. Level 4 – 150 yards – 100 yard carry
3. Level 5 – 200 yards – 125 yard carry
4. Level 6 – 1,801 to 2,300 yards – 150 yard carry
5. Level 7 – 2,301 to 2,600 yards – 175 yard carry
6. Level 8 – 2,601 to 2,900 yards – 200 yard carry
7. Level 9 – 2,901 to 3,200 yards – 225 yard carry
8. Level 10 – 3,201-plus yards – 260-plus yard carry

OPTIMISM: Once players start to build the wins of beating 36 from 25 yards, 50 yards in a nine-hole event their confidence increases. They start to identify themselves as someone who can perform and achieve. And once they start to identify themselves as that person they start doing activities that someone who performs and achieves on a regular basis does. For example, they start practicing more, they look for every area they can improve and use other role models as examples. If I start eating better, having a consistent pre-shot routine like the pro's do, that will help me perform and achieve at a higher level. And it is in these habits that they create that they move the needle forward in their skill which eventually leads to success.

References

ADM. (2021). *GOLF'S AMERICAN DEVELOPMENT MODEL*. PGA Coach. Retrieved September 13, 2022, from https://www.pga.coach/Golf's_American_Development_Model.pdf

Balyi, I. (2019). *LONG-TERM DEVELOPMENT*. Sport for Life. Retrieved September 13, 2022, from https://sportforlife.ca/wp-content/uploads/2019/06/Long-Term-Development-in-Sport-and-Physical-Activity-3.0.pdf

Cabot, R. (1940, June). A Long-Term Study of Children: The Cambridge-Somerville Youth Study. *Child Development*, *11*(2), 143-151. https://www.jstor.org/stable/1125845

Clear, J. (2018). *Atomic Habits: An Easy & Proven Way to Build Good Habits & Break Bad Ones*. Penguin Publishing Group.

Csikszentmihalyi, M. (2008). *Flow: The Psychology of Optimal Experience*. HarperCollins.

Eisenmann, J. (2018, March 19). *LTAD Part 1: Definition and History — Human Performance Blog · Volt Athletics*. Human Performance Blog · Volt Athletics. Retrieved September 13, 2022, from https://blog.voltathletics.com/home/2018/3/19/ltad-part-1-definition-and-history

Guadagnoli, M. A., & Lee, T. D. (2004). Challenge Point: A Framework for Conceptualizing the Effects of Various Practice Conditions in Motor Learning. *Journal of Motor Behavior*, *36*(2), 212-224. https://www.tandfonline.com/doi/abs/10.3200/JMBR.36.2.212-224

Highfield, I. (2019). *Golf Practice: How to Practice Golf and Take Your Range Game to the Course.* Game Like Training.

Matuszewski, E. (2022, March 31). *Record Beginners: Opportunities and Obstacles.* National Golf Foundation. Retrieved September 13, 2022, from https://www.ngf.org/record-beginners-opportunities-and-obstacles/

Miner, J. W. (2016, June 1). *Why 70 percent of kids quit sports by age 13.* The Washington Post. Retrieved September 13, 2022, from https://www.washingtonpost.com/news/parenting/wp/2016/06/01/why-70-percent-of-kids-quit-sports-by-age-13/

Ruger, H. A., & Bussenius, C. E. (1885). *Classics in the History of Psychology -- Ebbinghaus (1885/1913) Chapter 1.* Classics in the History of Psychology. Retrieved September 13, 2022, from http://psychclassics.yorku.ca/Ebbinghaus/index.htm

Shedloski, D. (2016, June 5). *William McGirt wins Memorial, ending 'years of...getting nose bloodied'.* Golf Digest. Retrieved September 13, 2022, from https://www.golfdigest.com/story/william-mcgirt-wins-memorial-ending-years-ofgetting-nose-bloodied

The truth about sports parents... (2016, June 10). YouTube. Retrieved September 13, 2022, from https://www.youtube.com/watch?v=u2LR4c3JsmU

ABOUT THE AUTHORS

RYAN DAILEY

Ryan has over 20 years of experience in the golf industry as a coach, educator and entrepreneur. He is a 18-year PGA member and holds two degrees, a Bachelors of Business Administration and a Masters of Business Administration, both from Campbell University.

His first experience in golf would have left most embarassed and looking for another sport. Rather he saw an opportunity. He stepped onto the local nine-hole course in Ray Brook, N.Y., at the age of 15 and proceeded to miss the ball multiple times, lose more than a dozen golf balls and shot close to 130... for 18 holes. However, he was hooked, and each time he went out, he got a little better, and the more he trained, the better he got.

Never good enough to make the college team as a walk-on at Campbell University, Ryan pursued a playing career after college in Dallas, Texas. After two years of rather dismal results, he turned his career towards teaching the game. He taught at the Hank Haney Golf Ranch in McKinney, Texas and at GolfTEC in North Dallas. He met David Orr at a seminar in North Carolina that would change his life and career trajectory. David encouraged him to apply for an open position to work alongside him at Campbell University's PGA Golf Management Program. Ryan jumped at the chance!

Ryan spent 10 years as a full-time faculty member and the Assistant Director of the PGA Golf Management Program at his alma mater, Campbell University. He mentored over 300 future PGA professionals, delivering the PGA Education program in the classroom and at the course. While at Campbell, he spent as much time as possible with David. David knew how to help people improve at golf like no one Ryan had ever met and he wanted to learn as much as he could from him.

While at Campbell, his hunger for learning combined with the fast approaching birth of his first son, led him to attend as many continuing education seminars taught by some of the brightest minds in golf coaching around the world as possible. He wanted to learn what the best strategies and training methods were that he could provide for his son and the local kids in the community.

He spent the years of 2007-2010 flying across the country on red eye flights to cram in as many seminars as possible while still fulfilling his duties as a faculty member. Dallas, Los Angeles, Chicago, Atlanta, Oceanside, etc. If a seminar was offered, he was going to it. Great information was passed on in these seminars, but no deliverable programs were ever shared that were simple to run.

Frustrated by this, Ryan feverishly took notes in hopes of someday being able to combine all of this great information into a simple program that anyone could run. It was on these trips that Ryan got to know Matt Reagan, a very motivated, focused and driven PGA Golf Management student at the University. Matt was one of the few students who took up the offer to join Ryan on these trips and showed a genuine interest in coaching.

The Great Recession that started in 2007 had a devastating impact on the University and specifically the golf course that they owned. In early 2010, when everyone was feeling the full force of the recession, the president of the University asked for ideas on how to get more people to use the golf course. It was perfect timing…serendipity some might say.

Ryan teamed up with Matt in 2010 to start to create a deliverable long term program at the University golf course, Keith Hills Golf

Club. They worked day and night over the next 13 years to refine, test and then refine again a program that would someday be used by coaches and students around the world.

From 2010-2016, Ryan would teach for the University during the day and coach during the evenings. In 2016, he left the University to focus full time on Operation 36 and continued in his Academy Director role at Keith Hills leading the Academy for 2 more years.

In 2018, he handed over the day-to-day coaching duties and focused the majority of his time on helping Matt at Operation 36 HQ and the corporate academy's they run under the name iGrow Golf in North Carolina/Virginia. He still loves coaching and from time to time can be found helping the coaching staff at Keith Hills in delivering classes, private lessons and 9-hole events.

The goal of Operation 36 is now to create 1,000,000 new golfers and be the #1 way to learn to play. Ryan and Matt are grateful to have almost 20 employees who day in and day out strive to improve the way the game of golf is learned.

Ryan lives in North Carolina with his wife, Melissa and three children. He caddies for his kids on a regular basis in the Operation 36 nine-hole events and enjoys seeing them make friends, improve their skills and learn valuable life lessons from this great game.

MATT REAGAN

Matt has over 15 years of experience in the golf industry as a coach, head professional, and entrepreneur. He is a 10-year PGA member and holds a Bachelors of Business Administration with a Major in Marketing, from Campbell University. 95% of his Professional career, Matt has been focused on coaching and developing what is now Operation 36 today.

Matt started playing golf later than most Professionals. He joined his High School golf team in upstate NY when he was 16. The sport hooked Matt to a point that it became a daily activity. Under the direction of his High School Golf Coach, Steve Thompson, Matt was able to go from not finishing a hole in a high school match, to being able to break even par for 9 holes by the time he was a senior in high school.

His passion for the sport led him to pursue a career in golf at Campbell Universities PGA Golf Management Program in 2007. This is where Matt met Ryan Dailey, the Assistant Director of the PGA Golf Management Program. Ryan was instrumental in helping guide Matt in his professional development. He really helped sparked Matt's interest in coaching and learning more about the golf swing.

Along the journey at Campbell and through multiple internships it became clear to Matt that he wanted to be a golf coach that specialized in developing junior golfers. Matt always felt that there could be a better plan to take someone from never playing and get them excited and skilled enough to play golf. There seemed to be a curriculum and development plan for juniors in every other sport, but not in golf.

While at school, Ryan and Matt had been researching junior golf development together through multiple certifications and educational seminars. In 2010, Ryan had an opportunity to start a junior golf program at Keith Hills Golf Club, Campbell University's Golf Club. Because of their shared interests, Ryan invited Matt to team up with him to begin the program. They got their first 3 students to sign up and began the partnership that led to what is Operation 36 Golf today.

After Matt graduated from Campbell a year later, he took the Head Professional job at Keith Hills Golf Club. Matt ran normal golf operations in the morning, and then would transition to coach and develop the Operation 36 Program in the afternoons with Ryan.

In 2013, Matt left the Head Professional position to focus full-time on Operation 36. In the years that followed he continued to develop the program with Ryan and started the program at 3 other locations in the Raleigh area where he would coach daily.

In 2016 they began licensing Operation 36 to other Golf Professionals. At this time, Matt stepped away from coaching and focused his full efforts on working with Ryan to develop the Operation 36 technology, curriculum, marketing, products and team that now service over 650 program locations and over 100,000 golfers around the world.

At his core, Matt loves solving problems and coaching others. He resides in North Carolina with his wife Kelsey and two children. He continues to co-lead the program with Ryan and is driven to accomplish the goal of creating 1,000,000 new golfers with Operation 36.

Printed in Great Britain
by Amazon